INSTANT POT VORTEX MINI AIR FRYER COOKBOOK:

A Comprehensive guide to 100+ Simple, Quick & Delicious Recipes to Fry, Bake and Grill Your Favourite Instant pot vortex mini air fryer Meals

Theresa T. Wilkey

Table of Contents

BOOK DESCRIPTION   5

INTRODUCTION   7

How Instant Vortex mini Air Fryer Works?   7
Ultimate Hints and Tips   8
Advantages Vortex mini Air Fryer   10
Care and Cleaning   11

CHAPTER 1: BREAKFAST RECIPES   13

1. Seed Porridge   13
2. Kale Breakfast Fritters   14
3. Herbed Breakfast Eggs   14
4. Eggs in Zucchini Nests   15
5. Early Morning Steak and Eggs   16
6. Breakfast Potatoes   17
7. Baked Potato Breakfast Boats   18
8. Greek Frittata   19
9. Mini Shrimp Frittata   20
10. Spinach and Mushroom Mini Quiche   21
11. Eggs in Avocado   22
12. Parmesan Zucchini Frittata   23
13. Fresh Herb Egg Cups   24
14. Bake Cheese Omelet   25
15. Feta Pepper Egg Muffins   26
16. Easy Scotch Eggs   27
17. Strawberry Toast   28
18. Onion and Cheese Omelet   29
19. Air Fried Shirred Eggs   30
20. Cheesy Hash Brown   31
21. Vegetable and Ham Omelet   32

CHAPTER 2: LUNCH RECIPES   33

22. Cheese Stuffed Green Peppers With Tomato Sauce   33
23. Basil White Fish   34
24. Cajun Salmon With Lemon   34
25. Lemon Salmon   35
26. Lemon Chicken Breasts   36
27. Almond Flour Battered Chicken Cordon Bleu   37
28. Almond Flour Coco-Milk Battered Chicken   37
29. Basil-Garlic Breaded Chicken Bake   38
30. BBQ Chicken Recipe from Greece   39
31. BBQ Pineapple 'n Teriyaki Glazed Chicken   40
32. Saucy Cod With Green Onions   41
33. Parmesan Tilapia Fillets   42
34. Party Cod Nuggets   43
35. Lemon Pepper Tilapia Fillets   44
36. Citrus Cilantro Catfish   45
37. Pork and Fruit Kebabs   45
38. Steak and Vegetable Kebabs   46
39. Spicy Grilled Steak   47

40.	CHICKEN RICE NOODLE SOUP	48
41.	JUICY PORK TENDERLOIN	49
42.	BAKED BEEF & BROCCOLI	50
43.	LEMON PEPPER PORK	51
44.	SESAME SEEDS BOK CHOY	51
45.	SPICY MUSHROOM SOUP	52
46.	BARBECUED LIME SHRIMP	53
47.	SPICY AIR-FRIED CHEESE TILAPIA	54
48.	CHEESE SALMON	54
49.	GREEK VEGETABLE SKILLET	55
50.	LIGHT HERBED MEATBALLS	56
51.	BROWN RICE AND BEEF-STUFFED BELL PEPPERS	57

CHAPTER 3: DINNER RECIPES — **59**

52.	SPICY PORK TENDERLOIN WITH BROCCOLI	59
53.	MEXICAN HOT MEATLOAF	60
54.	HONEY GLAZED SALMON	61
55.	CRISPY AIR FRIED SUSHI ROLL	62
56.	CRAB LEGS	63
57.	SPICY MACKEREL	64
58.	THYME SCALLOPS	65
59.	CHINESE STYLE COD	65
60.	MUSTARD SALMON	66
61.	CRUSTY PESTO SALMON	67
62.	BUTTERY COD	67
63.	SESAME TUNA STEAK	68
64.	GARLIC-ROASTED BELL PEPPERS	69
65.	ASPARAGUS WITH GARLIC	69
66.	CHEESY ROASTED SWEET POTATOES	70
67.	FENNEL OREGANO WEDGES	71
68.	PARSLEY KOHLRABI FRITTERS	72
69.	JUMBO SHRIMP	73
70.	TASTY CRAB PATTIES	74
71.	SUMMER EGGPLANT & ZUCCHINI	74
72.	ZUCCHINI HASSEL BACK	76
73.	SALTY LEMON ARTICHOKES	76
74.	ASPARAGUS & PARMESAN	77
75.	ONION GREEN BEANS	78
76.	LEMON GARLIC SHRIMP	79
77.	GARLICKY PORK BELLY WITH NEW POTATOES	80
78.	AIR FRIED CATFISH	81
79.	LEMON FISH FILLET	82
80.	COCONUT SHRIMP	82
81.	BAKED MAHI MAHI	83
82.	BAKED BASA	84
83.	BUFFALO WINGS	85
84.	SPANISH PORK KABOBS	86
85.	SIMPLE GREEK PORK SIRLOIN WITH TZATZIKI	87

CHAPTER 4: SNACKS AND DESSERTS — **89**

86.	SPICY CHICKPEAS	89
87.	ROASTED PEANUTS	90
88.	MAPLE CARROT FRIES	90
89.	SWEET POTATO FRIES	91
90.	CORN OKRA BITES	92
91.	SALTY POTATO CHIPS	93

92.	CORN & BEANS FRIES	94
93.	ROASTED CASHEWS	95
94.	FRENCH FRIES	95
95.	CHOCOLATE CHIP COOKIES	96
96.	RICOTTA CAKE	98
97.	ALMOND BROWNIE BOMBS	99
98.	CINNAMON NUT MUFFINS	100
99.	ROASTED PEANUTS	101
100.	ROASTED CASHEWS	101
101.	FRENCH FRIES	102
102.	ZUCCHINI FRIES	103
103.	SPICY CARROT FRIES	104
104.	AIR FRYER S'MORES	105
105.	DOUBLE-GLAZED CINNAMON BISCUIT BITES	106
106.	APPLE CIDER DONUTS	107
107.	MINI APPLE PIES	109
108.	ZUCCHINI FRIES	110
109.	WALNUT APPLE PEAR MIX	111
110.	WARM PEACH COMPOTE	112
111.	CRISPY ZUCCHINI CHIPS	113
112.	MIXED BERRIES CREAM	113
113.	PERFECT CINNAMON TOAST	114

CONCLUSION 116

BOOK DESCRIPTION

Are you looking for a combination air fryer and oven? Tired of switching between kitchen appliances? Then keep reading to find out the good news! The Instant Vortex mini Air Fryer Oven is now available on the market. This multifunctional kitchen miracle can provide a variety of cooking options in a single device. With its efficient electric heating system, you can now quickly bake, roast, air fry, broil, and dehydrate any type of food. This appliance is cost and time effective due to its user-friendly control system and multifunctional heating mechanism. If you enjoy cooking a variety of meals for yourself and your family, the Instant Vortex mini Air Fryer Oven is ideal for you.

The Instant Vortex mini Air Fryer Oven is not only great for everyday cooking, but it's also the perfect kitchen companion for large family gatherings and holidays. The Instant Vortex mini Air Fryer Oven is a lifesaver when it comes to cooking at home! You'll enjoy your nutritious meals more, save time and money, and your health will improve as a result.

This air fryer oven uses "rapid air technology" to quickly and healthily cook your favorite foods. You don't need a lot of oil to enjoy your favorite fried foods. By simply adding your ingredients to the cooking chamber, you can make healthy, air-fried foods in minutes. The Instant Vortex PRO Air Fryer Oven is a new "healthy frying" appliance for you!

The use of this kitchen appliance ensures that some of your favorite snacks and meals are made in a stress-free and hassle-free manner, which invariably validates its worth and gives you value for your money.

Remember that everyone starts out as a beginner; we all have to figure out what works best for us individually. Every time you make a new dish, you learn more and gain more experience. This is the healthiest way to prepare food that everyone in the family will enjoy and keep coming back for more of without even realizing it.

Whatever your reason for purchasing this book, it is uniquely designed to be both a beginner's guide for your appliance and a collection of recipes of varying complexity. It is an ideal, useful tool for anyone just getting started with their Instant Vortex mini or expanding their meal prep options.

This book covers:

- How Instant Vortex mini Air Fryer Works?

- Ultimate Tips And Tricks

- Benefits of the Vortex mini Air Fryer Oven

- Care and Cleaning

- Breakfast Recipes

- Lunch Recipes

- Dinner Recipes

- Snacks

- Desserts

And much more!!!

Get your copy now!!!

INTRODUCTION

How Instant Vortex mini Air Fryer Works?

The Instant Vortex Mini Air Fryer is a versatile cooking appliance that uses 1500 watts and has a maximum temperature of 400° F. The vortex air fryer plus cooks your food evenly from all sides by circulating very hot air into the food basket. You can fry a bowl of French fries with just 1 tablespoon of oil, and your vortex air fryer will make them crisp on the outside and tender on the inside.

The Instant Vortex Mini Air Fryer Plus has a large digital touch panel display that displays cooking time and temperature. The cooking basket for the Vortex air fryer is easily detachable from the main unit. Simply remove the food basket from the main unit, fill it with food, and replace it in its original position. Choose the desired program and press the start button. If the food needs to be turned or flipped, the vortex air fryer beeps for ten seconds before continuing the cooking process automatically.

The Instant Vortex mini Air Fryer is a cutting-edge cooking appliance that is simple to use, quick, easy to clean, portable, and versatile. Without the oil, hassles, and messiness associated with deep frying, you can air fry, bake, roast, dehydrate, and reheat your favorite meals. Crispy fries, onion rings, and chicken wings can all be air fried. In addition to cauliflower bites, garlicky potatoes, chicken nuggets, and shrimp skewers, this cooking appliance roasts. It also makes fluffy cinnamon rolls, mini pizzas, calzones, chewy brownie bites, and delectable cookies. You can also reheat your meals and dehydrate your fruit slices.

You can adjust the cooking time and temperature to have complete control while cooking. then save the presets so you can cook your meals by simply pressing a button Your food will begin to cook evenly and quickly as a powerful fan circulates the heat, giving it a delicious deep-fried taste and crunchy texture without using as much oil and grease as deep frying.

The Instant Vortex mini Air Fryer serves as a microwave, convection oven, and pizza oven all in one.

Less grease means less splatter. Say goodbye to your microwave, pizza oven, and convection oven; the Instant Vortex mini Air Fryer can do it all better.

The Vortex mini Air Fryer Oven has nine smart functions that are pre-programmed:

Air Fry is suitable for almost all deep-fried foods, including nuggets, French fries, chicken wings, and fritters.

Bake is great for making pastries, cookies, and cakes.

Roast - Use this preset to roast vegetables, poultry, pork, or fish.

Broil - This function cooks one side at a time, imparting a distinct grilled flavor; you can use it to finish oven-baked meats and fish that require a lower cooking temperature but benefit from crispy browning at the end.

Dehydrate - this is a great program for dried fruit, granola, jerky, and vegetables.

Reheat - With this handy feature, you can save money by reheating leftovers.

Proofing is an important step in baking because it is the process by which yeast is activated. Because it allows the dough to rise, this program is ideal for baking. Make authentic Italian focaccia and pizza, as well as traditional doughnuts and grandma's cinnamon rolls, with the rich flavor and fluffy texture you crave!

Toast is specially designed to make the best sandwiches ever!

Rotisserie is perfect for broiled or grilled meats, poultry, and seafood.

Ultimate Hints and Tips

Regardless of how simple this new technology is to use, there are a few things to keep in mind. First and foremost, read the appliance's user manual carefully and thoroughly.

Preheating should not be skipped; instead, before placing food in the oven, wait for the "Add Food" notification.

You want that delicious, crispy exterior, right? No worries; simply pat your dish dry before adding fat and aromatics. Culinary experts recommend starting with nonstick oil sprays (or misters) and then adding whatever aromatics or condiments you want (herbs, chile, garlic, mustard...).

Keep in mind that some foods contain natural fat, such as fatty cuts of meat and fatty fish, and thus do not require additional oil. Line a baking sheet with parchment paper or grease it.

When it comes to cooking time, make sure to check the doneness of your meal before removing it from the oven. Check on your food halfway through the cooking time. A variety of factors, such as the amount of food, its density, and so on, can influence the cooking time. If you're unsure about the cooking time, remember that while you can extend it, you can't save tasteless or dry items!

Remember that most meals require tossing or turning during the cooking process.

Use high-quality oils with a high smoke point when it comes to the oil. Applying too much oil, on the other hand, can result in excessive oil burning, so proceed with caution. Healthy fats include olive oil, coconut oil, peanut oil, avocado oil, butter, and ghee.

If you have time, blanch cruciferous vegetables like broccoli, cauliflower, cabbage, kale, Bok choy, and Brussels sprouts for 3 to 5 minutes before baking them. Then, before air frying your vegetables, drizzle them with herb vinaigrette (or olive oil). Cruciferous vegetables will retain their crunch and brightness this way.

To make deliciously crispy French fries, cut your potatoes into 1/4-inch sticks and soak them in cold water for 30 minutes. Using paper towels, drain and pat dry the potato sticks. Try not to cram the potato sticks into the cooking tray. At this point, place the fries on a cooling rack set over a roasting pan. While the potatoes are still warm, season with your preferred seasonings. A pro tip: add a few dashes of vinegar to the water with the potatoes to improve the flavor of your fries.

To get a crispier result, pat damp food items dry before cooking.

Finally, but not least, make use of the best products available!

People frequently believe that preparing nutritious and delectable meals necessitates extra effort. This is not true; all it takes is a change in your cooking and eating habits! I can also reduce my stress by using a professional kitchen tool. With my new air fryer, freshly prepared, home-cooked meals are only a few minutes away!

Advantages Vortex mini Air Fryer

The Vortex comes with ten smart programs pre-programmed for each of the cooking modes. This includes the default cooking temperatures and times for each of the cooking modes. This makes it very simple to use this multi-functional appliance because it eliminates the guesswork of determining which cooking mode to use and the optimal temperature for any given cooking mode.

The programming also tells you when to place the food inside the Vortex air fryer oven, when to turn food over or rotate the cooking trays, and when to remove the food from the air fryer oven.

Incredibly Versatile

There is currently no other appliance on the market that incorporates seven different cooking modes in one appliance. You would need several various appliances for the same functions that the Vortex offers.

Convenience

You do not have to go out to get fast food; you can make a healthier option at home. The rotisserie presents you with a crisp whole chicken and roast meat without a stove oven. You can switch instantly between cooking different types of food; there is no need to invest in several appliances.

Cooks Fast

The Vortex cooks faster, so you can have deep-fried tasting food much quicker than conventional deep-frying.

Quick and Easy to Clean

Cleaning the Vortex is not a major chore. There is no scrubbing with harsh chemicals, and all the accessories are dishwasher safe. Cleaning by hand is just as quick with a cloth and soapy water.

Health Benefits

There is no water involved in the cooking process; therefore, no loss of essential nutrients.

The food cooks fast, which means the food is not exposed to high heat for long periods, so the nutrients and vitamins are not depleted.

Minimal or no oil used in the cooking process; plus, no need to add fats or oil to prevent food drying out is a huge health benefit for everyone.

Energy Saving

The speed of the Vortex cooking brings about saving in electricity when compared to other cooking appliances.

Deep-Fried Taste

The air fryer crisps the food on the outside but keeps the food juicy; giving you great deep-fried tasting food without copious amounts of oil.

Multi-Use Rotisserie Basket, Fork, and Spit

The rotisserie basket is not only for making rotisserie chicken. You get all-over crisp roasts, vegetables, and sweet potato and potato fries. The spit and fork can handle any weight up to 4 lbs for roast pieces and whole chickens, and the basket and rotisserie fork rotates continuously during the cooking process for perfectly fresh food.

Standard Accessories

These are the standard accessories that come with your Vortex air fryer oven when you purchase it. Each fixture has a specific function and is designed specifically for this appliance.

Care and Cleaning

It is important that you clean the Air Fryer after using it. However, ensure that it is unplugged and allowed to cool before you commence the cleaning. When cleaning, do not use scouring pads, harsh chemical detergents, or powders to clean any of the components of the Air Fryer. Here are some of the best ways to clean the different parts of the Instant Vortex Air Fryer:

The cooking tray: It comes with a non-stick coating that can be damaged if you use cleaning utensils made of metal. Cleaning the Cooking Tray requires the use of a sponge or cloth, dish soap, and a warm water solution. Alternatively, you can just put it inside an automatic dishwasher.

The air fry basket: To clean the Air Fryer Basket, you will need a clot or sponge wit a warm water solution and dish soap. Be sure to remove all the food debris and grease. Avoid cleaning the basket inside an automatic dishwasher and avoid immersing the basket inside water or any liquid.

The cooking chamber: When cleaning the Cooking Chamber, use a cloth or sponge with a warm water solution and dish soap. You will need to spray the cooking chamber with a mixture of vinegar and baking soda in order to remove food residue and baked-on grease from it. If, however, the stains are too stubborn, you can allow the vinegar and baking soda mixture to sit on the stain for some time before scrubbing again.

The exterior: Use a soft, damp sponge or cloth to clean the exterior, then wipe it dry.

When you are done cleaning and drying all the parts of the Instant Vortex Air Fryer, place all the components back in their original positions.

CHAPTER 1: BREAKFAST RECIPES

1. Seed Porridge

Preparation Time: *10 minutes*

Cooking Time: *12 minutes*

Servings: 3

Ingredients:

1 tablespoon butter

¼ teaspoon nutmeg

1/3 cup heavy cream

1 egg

¼ teaspoon salt

3 tablespoons sesame seeds

3 tablespoons chia seeds

Directions:

1. Place the butter in your air fryer basket tray. Add the chia seeds, sesame seeds, heavy cream, nutmeg, and salt. Stir gently. Beat the egg in a cup and whisk it with a fork. Add the whisked egg to air fryer basket tray. Stir the mixture with a wooden spatula. Preheat your air fryer to 375°Fahrenheit. Place the air fryer basket tray into air fryer and cook the porridge for 12-minutes stir it about 3 times during the cooking process. Remove the porridge from air fryer basket tray immediately and serve hot!

Nutrition:

Calories 275

Fat 22.5g

Carbs 13.2g

Protein 7.9g

2. Kale Breakfast Fritters

Preparation Time: *8 minutes*

Cooking Time: *8 minutes*

Servings: 8

Ingredients:

12-ounces kale, chopped

1 teaspoon oil

1 tablespoon cream

1 teaspoon paprika

½ teaspoon sea salt

2 tablespoons almond flour

1 egg

1 tablespoon butter

½ yellow onion, diced

Directions:

1. Wash and chop the kale. Add the chopped kale to blender and blend it until smooth. Dice up the yellow onion. Beat the egg and whisk it in a mixing bowl. Add the almond flour, paprika, cream and salt into bowl with whisked egg and stir. Add the diced onion and blended kale to mixing bowl and mix until you get fritter dough. Preheat your air fryer to 360°Fahrenheit. Spray the inside of the air fryer basket with olive oil. Make medium-sized fritters with prepared mixture and place them into air fryer basket. Cook the kale fritters 4-minutes on each side. Once they are cooked, allow them to chill then serve.

Nutrition:

Calories 86

Fat 5.6g

Carbs 6.8g

Protein 3.6g

3. Herbed Breakfast Eggs

Preparation Time: *10 minutes*

Cooking Time: *17 minutes*

Servings: 2

Ingredients:

4 eggs

1 teaspoon oregano

1 teaspoon parsley, dried

½ teaspoon sea salt

1 tablespoon chives, chopped

1 tablespoon cream

1 teaspoon paprika

Directions:

1. Place the eggs in the air fryer basket and cook them for 17-minutes at 320°Fahrenheit. Meanwhile, combine the parsley, oregano, cream, and salt in shallow bowl. Chop the chives and add them to cream mixture. When the eggs are cooked, place them in cold water and allow them to chill. After this, peel the eggs and cut them into halves. Remove the egg yolks and add yolks to cream mixture and mash to blend well with a fork. Then fill the egg whites with the cream-egg yolk mixture. Serve immediately.

Nutrition:

Calories 136

Fat 9.3g

Carbs 2.1g

Protein 11.4g

4. Eggs in Zucchini Nests

Preparation Time: *10 minutes*

Cooking Time: *7 minutes*

Servings: 2

Ingredients:

4 teaspoons butter

½ teaspoon paprika

½ teaspoon black pepper

¼ teaspoon sea salt

4-ounces cheddar cheese, shredded

4 eggs

8-ounces zucchini, grated

Directions:

1. Grate the zucchini and place the butter in ramekins. Add the grated zucchini in ramekins in the shape of nests. Sprinkle the zucchini nests with salt, pepper, and paprika. Beat the eggs and pour over zucchini nests.

2. Top egg mixture with shredded cheddar cheese. Preheat the air fryer basket and cook the dish for 7-minutes. When the zucchini nests are cooked, chill them for 3-minutes and serve them in the ramekins.

Nutrition:

Calories 221

Fat 17.7g

Carbs 2.9g

Protein 13.4g

5. Early Morning Steak and Eggs

Preparation Time: *10 minutes*

Cooking Time: *30 minutes*

Servings: 4

Ingredients:

Cooking oil spray

4 (4-ounce) New York strip steaks

1 teaspoon granulated garlic, divided

1 teaspoon salt, divided

1 teaspoon freshly ground black pepper, divided

4 eggs

½ teaspoon paprika

Directions:

Insert the crisper plate into the basket and the basket into the unit. Preheat the unit by selecting air fry, setting the temperature to 360°F, and setting the time to 3 minutes, select start/stop to begin.

Once the unit is preheated, spray the crisper plate with cooking oil. Place 2 steaks into the basket; do not oil or season them at this time.

Select air fry, set the temperature to 360°F and set the time to 9 minutes, select start/stop to begin.

After 5 minutes, open the unit and flip the steaks. Sprinkle each with ¼ teaspoon of granulated garlic, ¼ teaspoon of salt, and ¼ teaspoon of pepper. Resume cooking until the steaks register at least 145°F on a food thermometer.

When the cooking is complete, transfer the steaks to a plate and tent with aluminum foil to keep warm. Repeat steps 2, 3, and 4 with the remaining steaks.

Spray 4 ramekins with olive oil. Crack 1 egg into each ramekin. Sprinkle the eggs with the paprika and remaining ½ teaspoon each of salt and pepper. Work in batches, place 2 ramekins into the basket.

Select BAKE, set the temperature to 330°F, and set the time to 5 minutes, select start/stop to begin. When the cooking is complete, and the eggs are cooked to 160°F, remove the ramekins and repeat step 7 with the remaining 2 ramekins.

Serve the eggs with the steaks.

Nutrition:

Calories 304

Fat 19g

Carbs 2g

Protein 31g

6. Breakfast Potatoes

Preparation Time: *10 minutes*

Cooking Time: *20 minutes*

Servings: *6*

Ingredients:

1½ teaspoons olive oil, divided, plus more for misting

4 large potatoes, skins on, cut into cubes

2 teaspoons seasoned salt, divided

1 teaspoon minced garlic, divided

2 large green or red bell peppers, cut into 1-inch chunks

½ onion, diced

Directions:

Lightly mist the fryer basket with olive oil.

In a medium bowl, toss the potatoes with ½ teaspoon of olive oil. Sprinkle with 1 teaspoon of seasoned salt and ½ teaspoon of minced garlic. Stir to coat.

Place the seasoned potatoes in the fryer basket in a single layer.

Cook for 5 minutes. Shake the basket and cook for another 5 minutes

Meanwhile, in a medium bowl, toss the bell peppers and onion with the remaining ½ teaspoon of olive oil.

Sprinkle the peppers and onions with the remaining 1 teaspoon of seasoned salt and ½ teaspoon of minced garlic. Stir to coat.

Add the seasoned peppers and onions to the fryer basket with the potatoes.

Cook for 5 minutes. Shake the basket and cook for an additional 5 minutes

Nutrition:

Calories 199

Fat 1g

Carbs 43g

Protein 5g

7. Baked Potato Breakfast Boats

Preparation Time: *10 minutes*

Cooking Time: *20 minutes*

Servings: 4

Ingredients:

2 large russet potatoes, scrubbed

Olive oil

Salt

Freshly ground black pepper

4 eggs

2 tablespoons chopped, cooked bacon

1 cup shredded cheddar cheese

Directions:

Poke holes in the potatoes with a fork and microwave on full power for 5 minutes. Turn potatoes over and cook an additional 3 to 5 minutes, or until the potatoes are fork-tender.

Cut the potatoes in half lengthwise and use a spoon to scoop out the inside of the potato. Be careful to leave a layer of potato so that it makes a sturdy "boat. "Lightly spray the fryer basket with olive oil. Spray the skin side of the potatoes with oil and sprinkle with salt and pepper to taste.

Place the potato skins in the fryer basket skin side down. Crack one egg into each potato skin. Sprinkle ½ tablespoon of bacon pieces and ¼ cup of shredded cheese on top of each egg. Sprinkle with salt and pepper to taste.

Air fry until the yolk is slightly runny, 5 to 6 minutes, or until the yolk is fully cooked, 7 to 10 minutes

Nutrition:

Calories 338

Fat15g

Saturated Fat 8g

Cholesterol 214mg

Carbs 35g

Protein 17g

Fiber 3g

Sodium: 301mg

8. Greek Frittata

Preparation Time: *10 minutes*

Cooking Time: *20 minutes*

Servings: 4

Ingredients:

Olive oil

5 eggs

¼ teaspoon salt

⅛ Teaspoon freshly ground black pepper

1 cup baby spinach leaves, shredded

½ cup halved grape tomatoes

½ cup crumbled feta cheese

Directions:

Spray a small round air fryer-friendly pan with olive oil.

In a medium bowl, whisk together eggs, salt, and pepper and whisk to combine.

Add the spinach and stir to combine.

Pour ½ cup of the egg mixture into the pan.

Sprinkle ¼ cup of the tomatoes and ¼ cup of the feta on top of the egg mixture.

Cover the pan with aluminum foil and secure it around the edges.

Place the pan carefully into the fryer basket.

Air fry for 12 minutes

Remove the foil from the pan and cook until the eggs are set, 5 to 7 minutes

Remove the frittata from the pan and place on a serving platter. Repeat with the remaining ingredients.

Nutrition:

Calories 146

Fat 10g

Carbs 3g

Protein 11g

Fiber 1g

9. Mini Shrimp Frittata

Preparation Time: *15 minutes*

Cooking Time: *20 minutes*

Servings: 4

Ingredients:

1 teaspoon olive oil, plus more for spraying

½ small red bell pepper, finely diced

1 teaspoon minced garlic

1 (4-ounce) can of tiny shrimp, Dry out

Salt

Freshly ground black pepper

4 eggs, beaten

4 teaspoons ricotta cheese

Directions:

Spray four ramekins with olive oil. In a medium skillet over medium-low heat, heat 1 teaspoon of olive oil. Add the bell pepper and garlic and sauté until the pepper is soft, about 5 minutes. Add the shrimp, season with salt and pepper, and cook until warm, 1 to 2 minutes. Remove from the heat.

Add the eggs and stir to combine. Pour one-quarter of the mixture into each ramekin.

Place 2 ramekins in the fryer basket and cook for 6 minutes. Remove the fryer basket from the air fryer and stir the mixture in each ramekin. Top each frittata with 1 teaspoon of ricotta cheese. Return the fryer basket to the air fryer and cook until eggs are set and the top is lightly browned, 4 to 5 minutes.

Repeat with the remaining two ramekins.

Nutrition:

Calories 114

Fat 7g

Carbs 1g

Protein 12g

10.   Spinach and Mushroom Mini Quiche

Preparation Time: *10 minutes*

Cooking Time: *15 minutes*

Servings: *4*

Ingredients:

1 teaspoon olive oil, plus more for spraying

1 cup coarsely chopped mushrooms

1 cup fresh baby spinach, shredded

4 eggs, beaten

½ cup shredded Cheddar cheese

½ cup shredded mozzarella cheese

¼ teaspoon salt

¼ teaspoon black pepper

Directions:

Spray 4 silicone baking cups with olive oil and set aside. In a medium sauté pan over medium heat, warm 1 teaspoon of olive oil. Add the mushrooms and sauté until soft, 3 to 4 minutes. Add the spinach and cook until wilted, 1 to 2 minutes Set aside.

In a medium bowl, whisk together the eggs, Cheddar cheese, mozzarella cheese, salt, and pepper. Gently fold the mushrooms and spinach into the egg mixture.

Pour ¼ of the mixture into each silicone baking cup. Place the baking cups into the fryer basket and air fry for 5 minutes. Stir the mixture in each ramekin slightly and air fry until the egg has set, an additional 3 to 5 minutes.

Nutrition:

Calories 183 Fat 13g

Carbs 3g

Protein 14g

Fiber 1g

11.   Eggs in Avocado

Preparation time: *8 minutes*

Cooking time: *15 minutes*

Servings: 2

Ingredients:

1 avocado, pitted

1/4 tsp. turmeric

1/4 tsp. black pepper, ground

1/4 tsp. salt

2 eggs

1 tsp. butter

1/4 tsp. flax seeds

Directions:

Take a shallow bowl and add the turmeric, butter, ground black pepper, salt, and flax seeds together. Shake gently to combine.

Cut the avocado into 2 halves.

Crack the eggs in a separate bowl.

Sprinkle the eggs with the spice mixture.

Place the eggs in the avocado halves.

Put the avocado boats in the air fryer.

Set the air fryer to 355°F and close it.

Cook the dish for 15 minutes or until the eggs are cooked to preference.

Serve immediately.

Nutrition:

Calories: 288

Fat: 26 g.

Fiber: 6.9 g.

Carbs: 9.4 g.

Protein: 7.6 g.

12.   Parmesan Zucchini Frittata

Preparation Time: 10 minutes

Cooking Time: 30 minutes

Servings: 4

Ingredients:

8 eggs

2 zucchinis, chopped and cooked

1 tbsp fresh parsley, chopped

3 tbsp parmesan cheese, grated

1 tsp garlic powder

Pepper

Salt

Directions:

In a large bowl, whisk eggs with garlic powder, pepper, and salt. Stir in parsley, cheese, and zucchini.

Pour egg mixture into the greased baking dish. Cover dish with foil.

Select Bake mode.

Set time to 30 minutes and temperature 350 F then press START.

The air fryer display will prompt you to ADD FOOD once the temperature is reached then place the baking dish in the air fryer basket.

Serve and enjoy.

Nutrition:

Calories 158

Fat 9.9 g

Carbohydrates 4.7 g

Sugar 2.6 g

Protein 13.8 g

13.   Fresh Herb Egg Cups

Preparation Time: 10 minutes

Cooking Time: 20 minutes

Servings: 6

Ingredients:

6 eggs

1 tbsp fresh parsley, chopped

1 tbsp chives, chopped

1 tbsp fresh basil, chopped

1 tbsp fresh cilantro, chopped

1/4 cup mozzarella cheese, grated

1 tbsp fresh dill, chopped

Pepper

Salt

Directions:

In a bowl, whisk eggs with pepper and salt. Add remaining ingredients and stir well.

Pour egg mixture into the silicone muffin molds.

Select Bake mode.

Set time to 20 minutes and temperature 350 F then press START.

The air fryer display will prompt you to ADD FOOD once the temperature is reached then place muffin molds in the air fryer basket.

Serve and enjoy.

Nutrition:

Calories 68

Fat 4.6 g

Carbohydrates 0.8 g

Sugar 0.4 g

Protein 6 g

14. Bake Cheese Omelet

Preparation Time: 10 minutes

Cooking Time: 25 minutes

Servings: 6

Ingredients:

8 eggs

1/4 cup cheddar cheese, shredded

2 tbsp green onions, chopped

1/4 tsp garlic powder

1/2 cup unsweetened almond milk

1/2 cup half and half

Pepper

Salt

Directions:

In a bowl, whisk eggs with milk, half and half, garlic powder, pepper, and salt. Stir in green onion and cheese.

Pour egg mixture into the greased 8-inch baking dish. Cover dish with foil.

Select Bake mode.

Set time to 25 minutes and temperature 350 F then press START.

The air fryer display will prompt you to ADD FOOD once the temperature is reached then place the baking dish in the air fryer basket.

Serve and enjoy.

Nutrition:

Calories 134

Fat 10 g

Carbohydrates 1.8 g

Sugar 0.6 g

Protein 9.3 g

15.   Feta Pepper Egg Muffins

Preparation Time: 10 minutes

Cooking Time: 20 minutes

Servings: 12

Ingredients:

4 eggs

1/2 cup egg whites

1 tsp garlic powder

2 tbsp feta cheese, crumbled

2 tbsp green onion, chopped

4 fresh basil leaves, chopped

1/4 cup unsweetened coconut milk

1 red bell pepper, chopped

Pepper

Salt

Directions:

In a bowl, whisk eggs, egg whites, milk, garlic powder, pepper, and salt.

Stir in cheese, bell pepper, green onion, and basil.

Pour egg mixture into the silicone muffin molds.

Select Bake mode.

Set time to 20 minutes and temperature 350 F then press START.

The air fryer display will prompt you to ADD FOOD once the temperature is reached then place muffin molds in the air fryer basket.

Serve and enjoy.

Nutrition:

Calories 46

Fat 3 g

Carbohydrates 1.5 g

Sugar 1 g

Protein 3.5 g

16.   Easy Scotch Eggs

Preparation time: *10 minutes*

Cooking time: *20 minutes*

Servings: 4

Ingredients:

1 lb. breakfast sausage, ground

3 tbsp. flour

4 hard-boiled eggs, peeled

1 egg

1 tbsp. water

3/4 cup panko bread crumbs

Directions:

In a bowl, mix the sausage and 1 tbsp. flour.

Divide the sausage mixture into 4 equal parts. Lay one hard-boiled egg in the center, then wrap the sausage around the egg, sealing completely. Repeat with remaining sausage parts and hard-boiled eggs.

In a small bowl, whisk the egg and water until smooth.

Place the remaining flour and bread crumbs into separate bowls large enough to dredge the sausage-wrapped eggs.

Dredge the sausage-wrapped eggs in the flour, then in the whisked egg, and finally coat in the bread crumbs.

Arrange them in the basket. Put the air fryer lid on and cook in the preheated instant vortex at 375°F for 20 minutes. Flip them over when the lid screen indicates "TURN FOOD" halfway through, or until the sausage is cooked to desired doneness.

Remove from the basket and serve on a plate.

Nutrition:

Calories: 509

Total fat: 16 g.

Net carbs: 2 g.

Fiber: 7 g.

Protein: 24 g.

Sugar: 16 g.

17.   Strawberry Toast

Preparation time: *10 minutes*

Cooking time: *8 minutes*

Servings: 4

Ingredients:

4 slices bread, 1/2-inch thick

1 cup sliced strawberries

1 tsp. sugar

Cooking spray

Directions:

On a plate, place the bread slices. Spray one side of each bread slice with cooking spray.

Arrange the bread slices (sprayed side down) in the air fryer basket. Evenly spread the strawberries onto them and sprinkle them with sugar.

Put the air fryer lid on and cook in the preheated instant vortex at 375°F for 8 minutes, or until the tops are covered with a beautiful glaze.

Remove from the basket and serve on a plate.

Nutrition:

Calories: 375

Total fat: 22 g.

Saturated fat: 5 g.

Total carbs: 2g.

Fiber: 4 g.

Protein: 14 g.

18. Onion and Cheese Omelet

Preparation Time: *5 minutes*

Cooking Time: 10 minutes

Servings: 2

Ingredients

2 eggs

2 tbsp. Grated cheddar cheese

1 tsp. Soy sauce

1/2 onion, sliced

1/4 tsp. Pepper

1 tbsp. Olive oil

Directions:

Whisk the eggs along with the pepper and soy sauce.

Three hundred fifty degrees preheat the air fryer.

Heat the olive oil and add the egg mixture and the onion.

Cook for 8 to 10 minutes.

Top with the grated cheddar cheese.

Nutrition:

Calories: 347

Fat: 23.2 g

Protein: 13.6 g

Carbs: 6 g

Fiber: 1.2 g

19.   Air Fried Shirred Eggs

Preparation Time: *6 minutes*

Cooking Time: 14 minutes

Servings: 2

Ingredients:

2 tsp. Butter for greasing

4 eggs, divided

2 tbsp. Heavy cream

4 slices ham

3 tbsp. Parmesan cheese

1/4 tsp. Paprika

3/4 tsp. Salt

1/4 tsp. Pepper

2 tsp. Chopped chives

Directions:

Preheat the air fryer to 360F.

Grease a pie pan with butter. Arrange the ham slices on the bottom of the pot to cover it completely.

Whisk one egg along with the heavy cream, salt, and pepper in a small bowl.

Pour the mixture over the ham slices.

Crack the other eggs over the ham. Sprinkle with parmesan cheese.

Cook for 14 minutes.

Season with paprika, garnish with chives, and serve with low carb bread.

Nutrition:

Calories: 279

Fat: 20 g

Protein: 20.8 g

Carbs: 1.8 g

Fiber: 0.2 g

20.   Cheesy Hash Brown

Preparation Time: *30 minutes*

Cooking Time: 7-10 minutes

Servings: 6

Ingredients:

1½ lbs. hash browns

6 bacon slices; chopped.

8 oz. cream cheese; softened

1 yellow onion; chopped.

6 eggs

6 spring onions; chopped.

1 cup cheddar cheese; shredded

1 cup almond milk

A drizzle of olive oil

Salt and black pepper to taste

Directions:

Heat your air fryer with the oil at 350°F. In a bowl, mix all other ingredients, except for the spring onions, and whisk well.

Add this mixture to your air fryer, cover and cook for 20 minutes.

Divide between plates, sprinkle the spring onions on top and serve.

Nutrition:

Saturated Fat 3.5g

Sugar 2g

Protein 8g

Total Carbohydrate 16g

Dietary Fiber 1g

21.   Vegetable and Ham Omelet

Preparation time: *5 minutes*

Cooking time: *20 minutes*

Servings: 6

Ingredients:

1/4 cup ham, diced

1/4 cup green or red bell pepper, cored and chopped

1/4 cup onion, chopped

1 tsp. butter

4 large eggs

2 tbsp. milk

1/8 tsp. salt

3/4 cup sharp cheddar cheese, grated

Directions:

Add the ham, bell pepper, onion, and butter into a 6×6×2-inch baking pan. Place the pan inside the air fryer basket.

Put the air fryer lid on and cook in the preheated instant vortex at 375°F for 6 minutes. Stir once halfway through the cooking time, or until the vegetables are soft.

In a bowl, whisk the eggs, milk, and salt until smooth and creamy. Gently pour over the ham and vegetables in the pan.

Put the air fryer lid on and cook at 375°F for about 13 minutes, or until the top begins to turn brown.

Top with the cheese and cook for 1 minute more, or until the cheese is bubbly and melted.

Remove from the basket and cool for 5 minutes before serving.

Nutrition:

Calories: 367

Total fat: 14 g.

Total carbs: 13 g.

Fiber: 6 g.

Protein: 18 g.

Sugar: 2 g.

CHAPTER 2: LUNCH RECIPES

22.   Cheese Stuffed Green Peppers With Tomato Sauce

Preparation time: *15 minutes*

Cooking time: *35 minutes*

Servings: 4

Ingredients:

2 cans green chili peppers

1 cup Cheddar cheese, shredded

1 cup Monterey Jack cheese, shredded

2 tbsp. all-purpose flour

2 large eggs, beaten

1/2 cup milk

1 can tomato sauce

Directions:

Preheat Instant Vortex on the "Air Fry" function to 380ºF.

Spray a baking dish with cooking spray. Take half of the chilies and arrange them in the baking dish. Top with half of the cheese and cover with the remaining chilies. In a medium bowl, combine eggs, milk, and flour and pour over the chilies.

Press "Start" and cook for 20 minutes. Remove the chilies and pour the tomato sauce over them; cook for 15 more minutes. Top with the remaining cheese and serve.

Nutrition:

Calories: 309

Carbs: 33 g.

Protein: 22 g.

Fat: 12 g.

23.   Basil White Fish

Preparation time: *10 minutes*

Cooking time: *20 minutes*

Servings: 4

Ingredients:

2 tbsp. fresh basil, chopped

2 garlic cloves, minced

1 tbsp. Parmesan cheese, grated

Salt and black pepper to taste

2 tbsp. pine nuts

4 white fish fillets

2 tbsp. olive oil

Directions:

Preheat Instant Vortex on the "Air Fry" function to 350ºF. Season the fillets with salt and pepper and place them in the basket. Drizzle with some olive oil and press "Start." Cook for 12–14 minutes.

In a bowl, mix basil, remaining olive oil, pine nuts, garlic, and Parmesan cheese and spread on the fish. Serve.

Nutrition:

Calories: 298

Carbs: 31 g.

Protein: 34 g.

Fat: 8 g.

24.   Cajun Salmon With Lemon

Preparation time: *5 minutes*

Cooking time: *10 minutes*

Servings: 1

Ingredients:

1 salmon fillet

1/4 tsp. brown sugar

Juice of 1/2 lemon

1 tbsp. Cajun seasoning

2 lemon wedges

1 tbsp. fresh parsley, chopped

Directions:

Preheat Instant Vortex on the "Bake" function to 350°F.

Combine sugar and lemon and coat in the salmon. Sprinkle with the Cajun seasoning as well.

Place parchment paper on a baking tray and press "Start." Cook for 14–16 minutes.

Serve with lemon wedges and chopped parsley.

Nutrition:

Calories: 221

Carbs: 11 g.

Protein: 12g.

Fat: 7 g.

25.   **Lemon Salmon**

Preparation time: *10 minutes*

Cooking time: *20 minutes*

Servings: 2

Ingredients:

2 salmon fillets

Salt to taste

Zest of 1 lemon

Directions:

Preheat the Instant Vortex oven for 14 minutes at 360°F.

Rub the fillets with salt and lemon zest. Place them in the frying basket and spray with cooking spray. Press "Start" and cook the salmon for 14 minutes at 360°F on the "Air Fry" function.

Serve with steamed asparagus and a drizzle of lemon juice.

Nutrition:

Calories: 332

Carbs: 41 g.

Protein: 14 g.

Fat: 10 g.

26.   Lemon Chicken Breasts

Preparation Time: *10 minutes*

Cooking Time: *30 minutes*

Servings: 4

Ingredients:

1/4 cup olive oil

3 tablespoons garlic, minced

1/3 cup dry white wine

1 tablespoon lemon zest, grated

2 tablespoons lemon juice

1 1/2 teaspoons dried oregano, crushed

1 teaspoon thyme leaves, minced

Salt and black pepper

4 skin-on boneless chicken breasts

1 lemon, sliced

Directions:

Whisk everything in a baking pan to coat the chicken breasts well.

Place the lemon slices on top of the chicken breasts.

Spread the mustard mixture over the toasted bread slices.

Press the "Power Button" of Air Fry Oven and turn the dial to select the "Bake" mode.

Press the Time button and again turn the dial to set the cooking time to 30 minutes.

Now push the Temp button and rotate the dial to set the temperature at 370 degrees F.

Once preheated, place the baking pan inside and close its lid.

Serve warm.

Nutrition:

Calories 388

Fat 8 g

Carbs 8 g

Protein 13 g

27.   Almond Flour Battered Chicken Cordon Bleu

Preparation Time: *5 minutes*

Cooking Time: *30 minutes*

Servings: *2*

Ingredients:

¼ cup almond flour

1 slice cheddar cheese

1 slice of ham

1 small egg, beaten

1 teaspoon parsley

2 chicken breasts, butterflied

Salt and pepper to taste

Directions:

Season the chicken with parsley, salt and pepper to taste.

Place the cheese and ham in the middle of the chicken and roll. Secure with a toothpick.

Soak the rolled-up chicken in egg and dredge in almond flour.

Place in the air fryer.

Cook for 30 minutes at 350F.

Nutrition:

Calories 1142

Carbs 5.5g

Protein 79.4g

Fat 89.1g

28.   Almond Flour Coco-Milk Battered Chicken

Preparation Time: *5 minutes*

Cooking Time: *30 minutes*

Servings: *4*

Ingredients:

¼ cup coconut milk

½ cup almond flour

1 ½ tablespoons old bay Cajun seasoning

1 egg, beaten

4 small chicken thighs

Salt and pepper to taste

Directions:

Preheat the air fryer for 5 minutes.

Mix the egg and coconut milk in a bowl.

Soak the chicken thighs in the beaten egg mixture.

In a mixing bowl, combine the almond flour, Cajun seasoning, salt and pepper.

Dredge the chicken thighs in the almond flour mixture.

Place in the air fryer basket.

Cook for 30 minutes at 350F.

Nutrition:

Calories 590

Carbs3.2g

Protein 32.5 g

Fat 38.6g

29. Basil-Garlic Breaded Chicken Bake

Preparation Time: *5 minutes*

Cooking Time: *30 minutes*

Servings: 2

Ingredients:

2 boneless skinless chicken breast halves (4 ounces each)

1 tablespoon butter, melted

1 large tomato, seeded and chopped

2 garlic cloves, minced

1 1/2 tablespoons minced fresh basil

1/2 tablespoon olive oil

1/2 teaspoon salt

1/4 cup all-purpose flour

1/4 cup egg substitute

1/4 cup grated Parmesan cheese

1/4 cup dry bread crumbs

1/4 teaspoon pepper

Directions:

In a shallow bowl, whisk well egg substitute and place flour in a separate bowl. Dip chicken in flour, then egg, and then flour. In a small bowl, whisk well the butter, bread crumbs and cheese. Sprinkle over chicken.

Lightly grease the baking pan of the air fryer with cooking spray. Place breaded chicken on the bottom of the pan. Cover with foil.

For 20 minutes, cook it at 390 F.

Meanwhile, in a bowl, whisk well the remaining ingredients.

Remove foil from the pan and then pour over the chicken the remaining Ingredients. Cook for 8 minutes. Serve and enjoy.

Nutrition:

Calories 311

Carbs 22.0g

Protein 31.0g

Fat 11.0g

30.   BBQ Chicken Recipe from Greece

Preparation Time: *5 minutes*

Cooking Time: *24minutes*

Servings: 2

Ingredients:

1 (8 ounces) container fat-free plain yogurt

2 tablespoons fresh lemon juice

2 teaspoons dried oregano

1-pound skinless, boneless chicken breast halves - cut into 1-inch pieces

1 large red onion, cut into wedges

1/2 teaspoon lemon zest

1/2 teaspoon salt

1 large green bell pepper, cut into 1 1/2-inch pieces

1/3 cup crumbled feta cheese with basil and sun-dried tomatoes

1/4 teaspoon ground black pepper

1/4 teaspoon crushed dried rosemary

Directions:

In a shallow dish, mix well rosemary, pepper, salt, oregano, lemon juice, lemon zest, feta cheese, and yogurt. Add chicken and toss well to coat. Marinate in the ref for 3 hours.

Thread bell pepper, onion, and chicken pieces in skewers. Place on skewer rack.

For 12 minutes, cook it on 360F. Turnover skewers halfway through cooking time. If needed, cook in batches.

Serve and enjoy.

Nutrition:

Calories 242

Carbs 12.3g

Protein 31.0g

Fat 7.5g

31.   BBQ Pineapple 'n Teriyaki Glazed Chicken

Preparation Time: *5 minutes*

Cooking Time: *20 minutes*

Servings: 2

Ingredients:

¼ cup pineapple juice

¼ teaspoon pepper

½ cup brown sugar

½ cup soy sauce

½ teaspoon salt

1 green bell pepper, cut into 1-inch cubes

1 red bell pepper, cut into 1-inch cubes

1 red onion, cut into 1-inch cubes

1 Tablespoon cornstarch

1 Tablespoon water

1 yellow red bell pepper, cut into 1-inch cubes

2 boneless skinless chicken breasts cut into 1-inch cubes

2 cups fresh pineapple cut into 1-inch cubes

2 garlic cloves, minced

Green onions for garnish

Directions:

In a saucepan, bring to a boil salt, pepper, garlic, pineapple juice, soy sauce, and brown sugar. In a small bowl, whisk well, cornstarch and water. Slowly stir into mixture in the pan while whisking constantly. Simmer until thickened, around 3 minutes. Save ¼ cup of the sauce for basting and set aside.

In a shallow dish, mix well chicken and the remaining thickened sauce. Toss well to coat. Marinate in the ref for a half hour.

Thread bell pepper, onion, pineapple, and chicken pieces in skewers. Place on skewer rack in the air fryer.

For 10 minutes, cook on 360F. Turnover skewers halfway through cooking time. And baste with sauce. If needed, cook in batches.

Serve and enjoy with a sprinkle of green onions.

Nutrition:

Calories 391

Carbs 58.7g

Protein 31.2g

Fat 3.4g

32.   Saucy Cod With Green Onions

Preparation time: *10 minutes*

Cooking time: *20 minutes*

Servings: 4

Ingredients:

4 cod fillets

2 tbsp. fresh coriander, chopped

Salt to taste

4 green onions, chopped

5 slices of ginger, chopped

5 tbsp. soy sauce

3 tbsp. olive oil

5 rock sugar cubes

1 cup water

Directions:

Preheat Instant Vortex on the "Air Fry" function to 390ºF. Season the cod with salt and coriander and drizzle with some olive oil. Place the fish fillet in the basket and press "Start." Cook for 15 minutes.

Heat the remaining olive oil in a skillet over medium heat and sauté green onions and ginger for 3 minutes. Add in soy sauce and the remaining ingredients and 1 cup of water. Bring to a boil and cook for 5 minutes until the sauce thickens. Pour the sauce over the fish and serve.

Nutrition:

Calories: 266

Carbs: 28 g.

Protein: 18 g.

Fat: 9 g.

33.   Parmesan Tilapia Fillets

Preparation time: *5 minutes*

Cooking time: *15 minutes*

Servings: 4

Ingredients:

3/4 cup Parmesan cheese, grated

1 tbsp. olive oil

1 tsp. paprika

1 tbsp. fresh parsley, chopped

1/4 tsp. garlic powder

1/4 tsp. salt

4 tilapia fillets

Directions:

Preheat Instant vortex on the "Air Fry" function to 350°F.

In a bowl, mix parsley, Parmesan cheese, garlic, salt, and paprika. Coat in the tilapia fillets and place them in a lined baking sheet. Drizzle with the olive oil press "Start." Cook for 8–10 minutes until golden. Serve warm.

Nutrition:

Calories: 145

Carbs: 43 g.

Protein: 21 g.

Fat: 17 g.

34.   Party Cod Nuggets

Preparation time: *15 minutes*

Cooking time: *25 minutes*

Servings: 4

Ingredients:

1 1/4 lb. cod fillets, cut into 4 chunks each

1/2 cup flour

1 egg

1 cup cornflakes

1 tbsp. olive oil

Salt and black pepper to taste

1 cup water

Directions:

Place the oil and cornflakes in a food processor and process until crumbed. Season the fish chunks with salt and pepper. In a bowl, beat the egg with 1 tbsp. of water.

Dredge the chunks in flour first, then dip in the egg, and finally coat with cornflakes. Arrange on a lined sheet and press "Start." Cook on the "Air Fry" function at 350ºF for 15 minutes until crispy. Serve.

Nutrition:

Calories: 391

Carbs: 56 g.

Protein: 11 g.

Fat: 2 g.

35.   Lemon Pepper Tilapia Fillets

Preparation time: *8 minutes*

Cooking time: *15 minutes*

Servings: 4

Ingredients:

1 lb. tilapia fillets

1 tbsp. Italian seasoning

2 tbsp. canola oil

2 tbsp. lemon pepper

Salt to taste

2–3 butter buds

Directions:

Preheat your Instant Vortex oven to 400ºF on the "Bake" function.

Drizzle tilapia fillets with canola oil. In a bowl, mix salt, lemon pepper, butter buds, and Italian seasoning; spread on the fish. Place the fillet on a baking tray and press "Start." Cook for 10 minutes until tender and crispy. Serve warm.

Nutrition:

Calories: 201

Carbs: 28 g.

Protein: 17 g.

Fat: 13 g.

36. Citrus Cilantro Catfish

Preparation time: *10 minutes*

Cooking time: *20 minutes*

Servings: 2

Ingredients:

2 catfish fillets

2 tsp. blackening seasoning

Juice of 1 lime

2 tbsp. butter, melted

1 garlic clove, mashed

2 tbsp. fresh cilantro, chopped

Directions:

In a bowl, blend garlic, lime juice, cilantro, and butter. Pour half of the mixture over the fillets and sprinkle with blackening seasoning.

Place the fillets in the basket and press "Start." Cook for 15 minutes at 360ºF on the "Air Fry" function. Serve the fish topped with the remaining sauce.

Nutrition:

Calories: 141

Carbs: 32 g.

Protein: 10 g.

Fat: 7 g.

37. Pork and Fruit Kebabs

Preparation Time: *15 minutes*

Cooking Time: *9-12 minutes*

Servings: 4

Ingredients:

⅓ cup apricot jam

2 tablespoons freshly squeezed lemon juice

2 teaspoons olive oil

½ teaspoon dried tarragon

1 (1-pound) pork tenderloin, cut into 1-inch cubes

4 plums, pitted and quartered

4 small apricots, pitted and halved

Directions:

In a large bowl, mix the jam, lemon juice, olive oil, and tarragon.

Add the pork and stir to coat. Let stand for 10 minutes at room temperature.

Alternating the items, thread the pork, plums, and -apricots onto 4 metal skewers that fit into the air fryer. Brush with any remaining jam mixture. Discard any remaining marinade.

Grill the kebabs in the air fryer for 9 to 12 minutes, or until the pork reaches 145°F on a meat thermometer and the fruit is tender. Serve immediately.

Nutrition:

Calories: 256

Fat; 5g

Protein: 24g

Carbohydrates: 30g

Fiber: 2g

Sugar: 22g

38.   Steak and Vegetable Kebabs

Preparation Time: *15 minutes*

Cooking Time: 5 to 7 minutes

Servings: 4

Ingredients:

2 tablespoons balsamic vinegar

2 teaspoons olive oil

½ teaspoon dried marjoram

⅛ teaspoon freshly ground black pepper

¾ pound round steak, cut into 1-inch pieces

1 red bell pepper, sliced

16 button mushrooms

1 cup cherry tomatoes

Directions:

In a medium bowl, stir together the balsamic vinegar, olive oil, marjoram, and black pepper. Add the steak and stir to coat. Let stand for 10 minutes at room temperature.

Alternating items, thread the beef, red bell pepper, mushrooms, and tomatoes onto 8 bamboos or metal skewers that fit in the air fryer.

Grill in the air fryer for 5 to 7 minutes, or until the beef is browned and reaches at least 145°F on a meat thermo-meter. Serve immediately.

Nutrition:

Calories: 194

Fat: 6g

Protein: 31g

Carbohydrates: 7g

Fiber: 2g

Sugar: 2g

39.   Spicy Grilled Steak

Preparation Time: *7 minutes*

Cooking Time: 6 to 9 minutes

Servings: 4

Ingredients:

2 tablespoons low-sodium salsa

1 tablespoon minced chipotle pepper

1 tablespoon apple cider vinegar

1 teaspoon ground cumin

⅛ teaspoon freshly ground black pepper

⅛ teaspoon red pepper flakes

¾ pound sirloin tip steak, cut into 4 pieces and gently pounded to about ⅓ inch thick

Directions:

In a small bowl, thoroughly mix the salsa, chipotle pepper, cider vinegar, cumin, black pepper, and red pepper flakes. Rub this mixture into both sides of each steak piece. Let stand for 15 minutes at room temperature.

Grill the steaks in the air fryer, two at a time, for 6 to 9 minutes, or until they reach at least 145°F on a meat thermometer.

Remove the steaks to a clean plate and cover with aluminum foil to keep warm. Repeat with the remaining steaks.

Slice the steaks thinly against the grain and serve.

Nutrition:

Calories: 160

Fat: 6g

Protein: 24g

 Carbohydrates: 1g

Fiber: 0g

Sugar: 0g

40.   Chicken Rice Noodle Soup

Preparation Time: *5 minutes*

Cooking Time: 10 minutes

Servings: 6

Ingredients:

6 cups chicken, cooked and cubed

3 tbsp. rice vinegar

2 ½ cups cabbage, shredded

2 tbsp. fresh ginger, grated

2 tbsp. soy sauce

3 garlic cloves, minced

8 oz. rice noodles

1 bell pepper, chopped

1 large carrot, peeled and sliced

6 cups chicken stock

2 celery stalks, sliced

1 onion, chopped

½ tsp. black pepper

Directions:

Add all ingredients into the air fryer and stir well.

Secure pot with lid and cook on manual high pressure for 10 minutes.

Quick release the pressure, then open the lid.

Stir well and serve.

Nutrition:

Calories – 306

Protein – 43.1 g.

Fat – 5.1 g.

Carbs – 18.7 g.

41.   Juicy Pork Tenderloin

Preparation Time: 10 minutes

Cooking Time: 20 minutes

Servings: 4

Ingredients:

1 1/2 lbs pork tenderloin

2 tbsp olive oil

1 tsp garlic powder

1 tsp Italian seasoning

1/4 tsp pepper

1 tsp sea salt

Directions:

Rub pork tenderloin with 1 tablespoon of olive oil.

Mix together garlic powder, Italian seasoning, pepper, and salt and rub over pork tenderloin.

Heat remaining oil in a pan over medium-high heat.

Add pork tenderloin in hot oil and cook until brown

Select Bake mode.

Set time to 15 minutes and temperature 400 F then press START.

The air fryer display will prompt you to ADD FOOD once the temperature is reached then place pork tenderloin in the air fryer basket.

Serve and enjoy.

Nutrition:

Calories 309

Fat 13.3 g

Carbohydrates 0.7 g

Sugar 0.3 g

Protein 44.7 g

42.   Baked Beef & Broccoli

Preparation Time: 10 minutes

Cooking Time: 25 minutes

Servings: 2

Ingredients:

1/2 cup broccoli florets

1/2 lb beef stew meat, cut into pieces

1 onion, sliced

1 tbsp vinegar

1 tbsp olive oil

Pepper

Salt

Directions:

Add meat and remaining ingredients into the large bowl and toss well.

Select Bake mode.

Set time to 25 minutes and temperature 390 F then press START.

The air fryer display will prompt you to ADD FOOD once the temperature is reached then place beef and broccoli in the air fryer basket.

Serve and enjoy.

Nutrition:

Calories 302

Fat 14.2 g

Carbohydrates 6.8 g

Sugar 2.8 g

Protein 35.7 g

43. Lemon Pepper Pork

Preparation Time: 10 minutes

Cooking Time: 15 minutes

Servings: 4

Ingredients:

4 pork chops, boneless

1 tsp lemon pepper seasoning

Salt

Directions:

Season pork chops with lemon pepper seasoning, and salt.

Select Air Fry mode.

Set time to 15 minutes and temperature 400 F then press START.

The air fryer display will prompt you to ADD FOOD once the temperature is reached then place pork chops in the air fryer basket.

Serve and enjoy.

Nutrition:

Calories 257

Fat 19.9 g

Carbohydrates 0.3 g

Sugar 0 g

Protein 18 g

44. Sesame Seeds Bok Choy

Preparation Time: *10 minutes*

Cooking Time: *6 minutes*

Servings: 4

Ingredients

bunches baby bok choy, bottoms removed and leaves separated

Olive oil cooking spray

1 teaspoon garlic powder

1 teaspoon sesame seeds

Directions:

1. Set the temperature of air fryer to 325 degrees F.

2. Arrange bok choy leaves into the air fryer basket in a single layer.

3. Spray with the cooking spray and sprinkle with garlic powder.

4. Air fry for about 5-6 minutes, shaking after every 2 minutes

5. Remove from air fryer and transfer the bok choy onto serving plates.

6. Garnish with sesame seeds and serve hot.

Nutrition:

Calories 26

Carbs 4g

Protein 2.5g

Fat 0.7g

45.   Spicy Mushroom Soup

Preparation Time: *5 minutes*

Cooking Time: 11 minutes

Servings: 2

Ingredients:

1 cup mushrooms, chopped

½ tsp. chili powder

2 tsp. garam masala

3 tbsp. olive oil

1 tsp. fresh lemon juice

5 cups chicken stock

¼ cup fresh celery, chopped

2 garlic cloves, crushed

1 onion, chopped

½ tsp. black pepper

1 tsp. sea salt

Directions:

Add oil into the air fryer and set on Sauté mode.

Add garlic and onion to the pot. Sauté for 5 minutes.

Add chili powder and garam masala. Cook for a minute.

Add remaining ingredients and stir well.

Secure pot with lid and cook on manual high pressure for 5 minutes.

Quick release the pressure, then open the lid.

Puree the soup using a blender and serve.

Nutrition:

Calories – 244

Protein – 3.9 g.

Fat – 22.8 g.

Carbs – 10.2 g.

46. Barbecued Lime Shrimp

Preparation Time: *5 minutes*

Cooking Time: *15 minutes*

Servings: 4

Ingredients:

4 cups of shrimp

1 ½ cups barbeque sauce

One fresh lime, cut into quarters

Directions:

1. Preheat your air fryer to 360°Fahrenheit. Place the shrimp in a bowl with barbeque sauce. Stir gently. Allow shrimps to marinade for at least 5-minutes. Place the shrimp in the air fryer and cook for 15-minutes. Remove from air fryer and squeeze lime over shrimps.

Nutrition:

Calories: 289,

Total Fat: 9.8g,

Carbs: 8.7g,

Protein: 14.9g

47. Spicy Air-Fried Cheese Tilapia

Preparation Time: *5minutes*

Cooking Time: *10 minutes*

Servings: 4

Ingredients:

1 lb. tilapia fillets

One tablespoon olive oil

Salt and pepper to taste

Two teaspoons paprika

¾ cup parmesan cheese, grated

Directions:

1. Preheat your air fryer to 400°Fahrenheit. Mix the parmesan cheese, paprika, salt, and pepper. Drizzle olive oil over the tilapia fillets and coat with paprika and cheese mixture. Place the coated tilapia fillets on aluminum foil. Put into the air fryer and cook for 10-minutes.

Nutrition:

Calories: 289,

Total Fat: 8.9g,

Carbs: 7.8g,

Protein: 14.9g

48. Cheese Salmon

Preparation Time: *4 minutes*

Cooking Time: *11 minutes*

Servings: 6

Ingredients:

2 lbs. salmon fillet

Salt and pepper to taste

½ cup parmesan cheese, grated

¼ cup parsley, fresh, chopped

Two garlic cloves, minced

Directions:

1. Preheat your air fryer to 350°Fahrenheit. Put the salmon skin side facing down on aluminum foil and cover with another piece of foil. Cook salmon for 10-minutes. Remove the salmon from foil and top it with minced garlic, parsley, parmesan cheese, and pepper. Return salmon to air fryer for 1-minute cook time.

Nutrition:

Calories: 297,

Total Fat: 9.5g,

Carbs: 8.3g,

Protein: 14.9g

49.　　Greek Vegetable Skillet

Preparation Time: *10 minutes*

Cooking Time: 9 to 19 minutes

Servings: 4

Ingredients:

½ pound 96 percent lean ground beef

2 medium tomatoes, chopped

1 onion, chopped

2 garlic cloves, minced

2 cups fresh baby spinach

2 tablespoons freshly squeezed lemon juice

⅓ cup low-sodium beef broth

2 tablespoons crumbled low-sodium feta cheese

Directions:

In a 6-by-2-inch metal pan, crumble the beef. Cook in the air fryer for 3 to 7 minutes, stirring once during cooking until browned. Drain off any fat or liquid.

Add the tomatoes, onion, and garlic to the pan. Air-fry for 4 to 8 minutes more, or until the onion is tender.

Add the spinach, lemon juice, and beef broth. Air-fry for 2 to 4 minutes more, or until the spinach is wilted.

Sprinkle with the feta cheese and serve immediately.

Nutrition:

Calories: 97

Fat: 1g

Protein: 15g

Carbohydrates: 5g

Fiber: 1g

Sugar: 2g

50.   Light Herbed Meatballs

Preparation Time: *10 minutes*

Cooking Time: 12 to 17 minutes

Servings: 24

Ingredients:

1 medium onion, minced

2 garlic cloves, minced

1 teaspoon olive oil

1 slice low-sodium whole-wheat bread, crumbled

3 tablespoons 1 percent milk

1 teaspoon dried marjoram

1 teaspoon dried basil

1-pound 96 percent lean ground beef

Directions:

In a 6-by-2-inch pan, combine the onion, garlic, and olive oil. Air-fry for 2 to 4 minutes, or until the vegetables are crisp-tender.

Transfer the vegetables to a medium bowl, and add the bread crumbs, milk, marjoram, and basil. Mix well.

Add the ground beef. With your hands, work the mixture gently but thoroughly until combined. Form the meat mixture into about 24 (1-inch) meatballs.

Bake the meatballs, in batches, in the air fryer basket for 12 to 17 minutes, or until they reach 160°F on a meat thermometer. Serve immediately.

Nutrition:

Calories: 190

Fat: 6g

Protein: 25g

Carbohydrates: 8g

Fiber: 1g;

Sugar: 2g

51.   Brown Rice and Beef-Stuffed Bell Peppers

Preparation Time: *10 minutes*

Cooking Time: 11 to 16 minutes

Servings: 4

Ingredients:

4 medium bell peppers, any colors, rinsed, tops removed

1 medium onion, chopped

½ cup grated carrot

2 teaspoons olive oil

2 medium beefsteak tomatoes, chopped

1 cup cooked brown rice

1 cup chopped cooked low-sodium roast beef

1 teaspoon dried marjoram

Directions:

Remove the stems from the bell pepper tops and chop the tops.

In a 6-by-2-inch pan, combine the chopped bell pepper tops, onion, carrot, and olive oil. Cook for 2 to 4 minutes, or until the vegetables are crisp-tender.

Transfer the vegetables to a medium bowl. Add the -tomatoes, brown rice, roast beef, and marjoram. Stir to mix.

Stuff the vegetable mixture into the bell peppers. Place the bell peppers in the air fryer basket. Bake for 11 to 16 minutes, or until the peppers are tender and the filling is hot. Serve immediately.

Nutrition:

Calories: 206

Fat: 6g

Protein: 18g

Carbohydrates: 20g

Fiber: 3g

Sugar: 5g

CHAPTER 3: DINNER RECIPES

52.   Spicy Pork Tenderloin With Broccoli

Preparation time: *20 minutes*

Cooking time: *35 minutes*

Servings: 4

Ingredients:

1 package (1 1/2 lb.) pork tenderloin, trimmed

1 tsp. mustard, ground

1/4 tsp. garlic powder

2 tbsp. brown sugar

1 tbsp. smoked paprika

1/4 tsp. cayenne pepper (optional)

1 tbsp. olive oil

4 cups broccoli, chopped into florets

1 tbsp. olive oil

Salt and black pepper, to taste

Directions:

In a bowl, put in the ground mustard, garlic powder, brown sugar, paprika, cayenne pepper, salt, and pepper, stir to mix well. Reserve.

Place the pork tenderloin on a clean working surface. Rub the tenderloin with olive oil on both sides, then dredge it in the mustard mixture to coat well. Let it sit for 5 minutes.

Gently arrange the tenderloin in the air fryer basket, and cook in the preheated instant vortex at 400°F for 10 minutes or until cooked through. Flip the tenderloin when the lid indicates "TURN FOOD" halfway through the cooking.

In the meantime, in a microwave-safe bowl, put in the broccoli and microwave on high for 3 minutes or until soft, then remove the broccoli from the microwave to a large dish, drizzle with olive oil and sprinkle with salt and pepper, toss to coat well. Reserve.

Remove the tenderloin from the basket to a clean working surface. Allow cooling for 10 minutes. Meanwhile, transfer the broccoli to the air fryer basket and cook in the preheated instant vortex at 400°F for 10 minutes. Give the basket a shake when the lid indicates "TURN FOOD" halfway through the cooking.

Remove the cooked broccoli from the basket to a large dish. Slice the cooled tenderloin and serve with broccoli.

Nutrition:

Calories: 270

Total fat: 11.1 g.

Carbs: 14 g.

Protein: 29.5 g.

53. **Mexican Hot Meatloaf**

Preparation time: *15 minutes*

Cooking time: *35 minutes*

Servings: 4

Ingredients:

1/2 lb. veal, ground

1/2 lb. pork, ground

2 tsp. chipotle sauce, gluten-free

1/4 cup cilantro, chopped

1/4 cup bread crumbs, gluten-free

1 large egg, beaten

2 spring onions, medium-sized, diced

Sriracha salt and ground black pepper, to taste

1/2 cup ketchup

1 tsp. blackstrap molasses

1 tsp. olive oil

Cooking spray

Directions:

In a bowl, mix the chipotle chili sauce, ketchup, molasses, and olive oil. Reserve under room temperature.

Combine the veal and pork on a clean working surface.

Make a well in the middle of the meat mixture, then put in the cilantro, bread crumbs, beaten egg, spring onion, Sriracha salt, and black pepper. Combine all of them well with your hands.

Shape the mixture into a loaf. Grease your hands with cooking spray to avoid a sticky situation. Arrange the meatloaf in a 6×6×2-inch baking pan.

Arrange the baking pan in the air fryer basket. Put the air fryer lid on and cook in the preheated instant vortex at 400°F for 25 minutes.

Remove the baking pan from the basket and pour the ketchup mixture on top of the meatloaf to cover generously.

Arrange the baking pan back to the basket and bake for another 7 minutes or until an instant-read thermometer registers at least 160°F.

Let the meatloaf stand in the basket for 5 minutes, then remove the meatloaf from the basket and cool for 5 minutes. Slice to serve.

Nutrition:

Calories: 272

Fat: 14.4 g.

Carbs: 13.3 g.

Protein: 22.1 g.

54.　　Honey Glazed Salmon

Preparation time: *5 minutes*

Cooking time: *13 minutes*

Servings: 2

Ingredients:

1 tsp. water

3 tsp. rice wine vinegar

6 tbsp. soy sauce, low-sodium

6 tbsp. raw honey

2 salmon fillets

Directions:

Combine water, vinegar, honey, and soy sauce together. Pour half of this mixture into a bowl.

Place salmon in one bowl of marinade and let chill 2 hours.

Ensure your air fryer is preheated to 356ºF and add salmon.

Cook 8 minutes, flipping halfway through. Baste salmon with some of the remaining marinade mixture and cook another 5 minutes.

To make a sauce to serve salmon with, pour remaining marinade mixture into a saucepan, heating till simmering. Let simmer 2 minutes. Serve drizzled over salmon!

Nutrition:

Calories: 390

Fat: 8 g.

Protein: 16 g.

Sugar: 5 g.

55.   **Crispy Air Fried Sushi Roll**

Preparation time: *15 minutes*

Cooking time: *10 minutes*

Servings: 12

Ingredients:

Kale Salad:

1 tbsp. sesame seeds

3/4 tsp. soy sauce

1/4 tsp. ginger

1/8 tsp. garlic powder

3/4 tsp. toasted sesame oil

1/2 tsp. rice vinegar

1 1/2 cup chopped kale

Sushi Rolls:

1/2 avocado, sliced

3 sheets sushi nori

1 batch cauliflower rice

Sriracha Mayo:

Sriracha sauce

1/4 cup vegan mayo

Coating:

1/2 cup panko breadcrumbs

Directions:

Combine all of the kale salad ingredients, tossing well. Set to the side.

Layout a sheet of nori and spread a handful of rice on it. Then place 2–3 tbsp. of kale salad over rice, followed by avocado. Roll up sushi.

To make mayo, whisk mayo ingredients together until smooth.

Add breadcrumbs to a bowl. Coat sushi rolls in crumbs till coated and add to the air fryer.

Cook rolls 10 minutes at 390ºF, shaking gently at 5 minutes.

Slice each roll into 6–8 pieces and enjoy!

Nutrition:

Calories: 267

Fat: 13 g.

Protein: 6 g.

Sugar: 3 g.

56.   Crab Legs

Preparation time: *5 minutes*

Cooking time: *20 minutes*

Servings: 3

Ingredients:

3 lb. crab legs

1/4 cup salted butter, melted and divided

1/2 lemon, juiced

1/4 tsp. garlic powder

Directions:

In a bowl, toss the crab legs and 2 tbsp. of the melted butter. Place the crab legs in the basket of the fryer.

Cook at 400°F for 15 minutes, giving the basket a good shake halfway through.

Combine the remaining butter with lemon juice and garlic powder.

Crack open the cooked crab legs and remove the meat. Serve with the butter dip on the side and enjoy!

Nutrition:

Calories: 392

Fat: 10 g.

Protein: 18 g.

Sugar: 8 g.

57.   Spicy Mackerel

Preparation Time: *5 minutes*

Cooking Time: 10 minutes

Servings: 4

Ingredients:

2 mackerel fillets

2 tbsp. red chili flakes

2 tsp. garlic, minced

1 tsp. lemon juice

Directions:

Season the mackerel fillets with red pepper flakes, minced garlic, and a drizzle of lemon juice.

Allow sitting for five minutes.

Preheat your fryer at 350°F.

Cook the mackerel for five minutes before opening the drawer, flipping the fillets, and allowing it to cook on the other side for another five minutes.

Plate the fillets, making sure to spoon any remaining juice over them before serving.

Nutrition:

Calories 393 Fat 12

Carbs 13 Protein 35

58. Thyme Scallops

Preparation Time: *5 minutes*

Cooking Time: 10 minutes

Servings: 4

Ingredients:

1 lb. scallops

Salt and pepper

½ tbsp. butter

½ cup thyme, chopped

Directions:

Wash the scallops and dry them completely. Season with pepper and salt, then set aside while you prepare the pan.

Grease a foil pan in several spots with the butter and cover the bottom with the thyme. Place the scallops on top.

Preheat the fryer at 400°F and set the rack inside.

Place the foil pan on the rack and allow to cook for seven minutes.

Take care when removing the pan from the fryer and transfer the scallops to a serving dish.

Spoon any remaining butter in the pan over the fish and enjoy.

Nutrition:

Calories 454

Fat 18

Carbs 27

Protein 34

59. Chinese Style Cod

Preparation Time: *5 minutes*

Cooking Time: 10 minutes

Servings: 2

Ingredients:

2 medium cod fillets; boneless

1 tbsp. light soy sauce

1/2 tsp. ginger; grated

1 tsp. peanuts; crushed

2 tsp. garlic powder

Directions:

Put fish fillets in a heat proof dish that fits your air fryer, add garlic powder, soy sauce, and ginger; toss well, put in your air fryer, and cook at 350 °F for 10 minutes.

Divide fish on plates, sprinkle peanuts on top and serve.

Nutrition:

Calories: 254;Fat: 10;

Fiber: 11;

Carbs: 14;

Protein: 23

60.   **Mustard Salmon**

Preparation Time: *5 minutes*

Cooking Time: 10 minutes

Servings: 4

Ingredients:

1 big salmon fillet; boneless

2 tbsp. mustard

1 tbsp. coconut oil

1 tbsp. maple extract

Salt and black pepper to the taste

Directions:

In a bowl, mix maple extract with mustard, whisk well, season salmon with salt and pepper, and brush salmon with this mix.

Spray some cooking spray over fish; place in your air fryer and cook at 370 °F for 10 minutes; flipping halfway. Serve with a tasty side salad.

Nutrition:

Calories: 300;

Fat: 7;

Fiber: 14;

Carbs: 16;

Protein: 20

61.   Crusty Pesto Salmon

Preparation time: *5 minutes*

Cooking time: *15 minutes*

Servings: 2

Ingredients:

1/4 cup spinach, roughly chopped

1/4 cup pesto

2 (4-oz.) salmon fillets

2 tbsp. unsalted butter, melted

Directions:

Mix the spinach and pesto.

Place the salmon fillets in a round baking dish, roughly 6-inch in diameter.

Brush the fillets with butter, followed by the pesto mixture, ensuring to coat both the top and bottom. Put the baking dish inside the fryer.

Cook for 12 minutes at 390°F.

The salmon is ready when it flakes easily when prodded with a fork. Serve warm.

Nutrition:

Calories: 290

Fat: 11 g.

Protein: 20 g.

Sugar: 9 g.

62.   Buttery Cod

Preparation time: *10 minutes*

Cooking time: *12 minutes*

Servings: 2

Ingredients:

2 (4 oz.) cod fillets

2 tbsp. salted butter, melted

1 tsp. Old Bay® seasoning

1/2 lemon, medium-sized, sliced

Directions:

Place the cod fillets in a baking dish.

Brush with melted butter, season with Old Bay®, and top with some lemon slices.

Wrap the fish in aluminum foil oand put it into your fryer.

Cook for 8 minutes at 350°F.

The cod is ready when it flakes easily. Serve hot.

Nutrition:

Calories: 394

Fat: 5 g.

Protein: 12 g.

Sugar: 4 g.

63.   Sesame Tuna Steak

Preparation time: *5 minutes*

Cooking time: *12 minutes*

Servings: 2

Ingredients:

1 tbsp. coconut oil, melted

2 (6 oz.) tuna steaks

1/2 tsp. garlic powder

2 tsp. black sesame seeds

2 tsp. white sesame seeds

Directions:

Apply the coconut oil to the tuna steaks with a brunch, then season with garlic powder.

Combine the black and white sesame seeds. Embed them in the tuna steaks, covering the fish all

over. Place the tuna into your air fryer.

Cook for 8 minutes at 400°F, turning the fish halfway through.

The tuna steaks are ready when they have reached a temperature of 145°F. Serve straight away.

Nutrition:

Calories: 160

Fat: 6 g.

Protein: 26 g.

Sugar: 7 g.

64.   Garlic-Roasted Bell Peppers

Preparation Time: *5 minutes*

Cooking Time: 20 minutes

Servings: 4

Ingredients:

4 bell peppers, any colors, stemmed, seeded, membranes removed, and cut into fourths

1 teaspoon olive oil

4 garlic cloves, minced

½ teaspoon dried thyme

Directions:

Put the peppers in the basket of the air fryer and drizzle with olive oil. Toss gently. Roast for 15 minutes.

Sprinkle with garlic and thyme. Roast for 3 to 5 minutes more, or until tender. Serve immediately.

Nutrition:

Calories: 36;

Fat: 1g

Protein: 1g;

Carbohydrates: 5g;

Fiber: 2g;

65.   Asparagus with Garlic

Preparation Time: *5 minutes*

Cooking Time: 10 minutes

Servings: 4

Ingredients:

1-pound asparagus, rinsed, ends snapped off where they naturally break (see Tip)

2 teaspoons olive oil

3 garlic cloves, minced

2 tablespoons balsamic vinegar

½ teaspoon dried thyme

Directions:

In a huge bowl, mix the asparagus with olive oil. -Transfer to the air fryer basket.

Sprinkle with garlic. Roast for 4 to 5 minutes for crisp-tender or for 8 to 11 minutes for asparagus that is crisp on the outside and tender on the inside.

Drizzle with the balsamic vinegar and sprinkle with the thyme leaves. Serve immediately.

Nutrition:

Calories: 41;

Fat: 1g

Protein: 3g;

Carbohydrates: 6g;

Sodium: 3mg;

66. **Cheesy Roasted Sweet Potatoes**

Preparation Time: *5 minutes*

Cooking Time: 20 minutes

Servings: 4

Ingredients:

2 large sweet potatoes, peeled and sliced

1 teaspoon olive oil

1 tablespoon white balsamic vinegar

1 teaspoon dried thyme

¼ cup grated Parmesan cheese

Directions:

In a big bowl, shower the sweet potato slices with olive oil and toss.

Sprinkle with the balsamic vinegar and thyme and toss again.

Sprinkle the potatoes with the Parmesan cheese and toss to coat.

Roast the slices, in batches, in the air fryer basket for 18 to 23 minutes, tossing the sweet potato slices in the basket once during cooking, until tender.

Repeat with the remaining sweet potato slices. Serve immediately.

Nutrition:

Calories: 100;

Fat: 3g

Protein: 4g;

Carbohydrates: 15g;

Sodium: 132mg;

67.   **Fennel Oregano Wedges**

Preparation Time: *15 minutes*

Cooking Time: *6 minutes*

Servings: 4

Ingredients:

1 teaspoon stevia extract

½ teaspoon fresh thyme

½ teaspoon salt

1 teaspoon olive oil

14 oz. fennel

1 teaspoon butter

1 teaspoon dried oregano

½ teaspoon chili flakes

Directions:

1. Slice the fennel into wedges. Melt the butter. Combine the butter, olive oil, dried oregano, and chili flakes in a bowl.

2. Combine well.

3. Add salt, fresh thyme, and stevia extract. Whisk gently.

4. Brush the fennel wedges with the mixture. Preheat the air fryer to 370 F.

5. Place the fennel wedges in the air fryer rack.

6. Cook the fennel wedges for 3 minutes on each side.

Nutrition:

Calories 41

Fat 1.9

Carbs 6.1

Protein 1

68.   Parsley Kohlrabi Fritters

Preparation Time: *10 minutes*

Cooking Time: *7 minutes*

Servings: 4

Ingredients:

oz. kohlrabi

1 egg

1 tablespoon almond flour

½ teaspoon salt

1 teaspoon olive oil

1 teaspoon ground black pepper

1 tablespoon dried parsley

¼ teaspoon chili pepper

Directions:

1. Peel the kohlrabi and grate it. Combine the grated kohlrabi with salt, ground black pepper, dried parsley, and chili pepper.

2. Crack the egg into the mixture and whisk it. Make medium fritters from the mixture.

3. Preheat the air fryer to 380 F. Grease the air fryer basket tray with olive oil and place the fritters inside. Cook the fritters for 4 minutes Turn the fritters and cook for 3 minutes more. Allow to cool slightly before serving.

Nutrition:

Calories 66

Fat 4.7

Carbs 4.4

Protein 3.2

69. Jumbo Shrimp

Preparation Time: 10 minutes

Cooking Time: 6 minutes

Servings: 4

Ingredients:

1 lb jumbo shrimp

1 tsp steak seasoning

1/4 tsp crushed red pepper flakes

2 garlic cloves, minced

2 tsp olive oil

1 tbsp parsley, chopped

2 tsp lemon juice

1 tsp lemon zest

Directions:

In a bowl, toss shrimp with parsley, lemon juice, lemon zest, steak seasoning, red pepper flakes, garlic, and olive oil.

Select Air Fry mode.

Set time to 6 minutes and temperature 400 F then press START.

The air fryer display will prompt you to ADD FOOD once the temperature is reached then add shrimp in the air fryer basket.

Serve and enjoy.

Nutrition:

Calories 105

Fat 2.4 g

Carbohydrates 0.8 g

Sugar 2.2 g

Protein 20.4 g

70.   Tasty Crab Patties

Preparation Time: 10 minutes

Cooking Time: 10 minutes

Servings: 4

Ingredients:

8 oz crab meat

2 tbsp mayonnaise

2 green onion, chopped

1/4 cup bell pepper, chopped

1 tsp old bay seasoning

1 tbsp Dijon mustard

2 tbsp almond flour

Pepper

Salt

Directions:

Add all ingredients into the mixing bowl and mix until well combined.

Make 4 equal shapes of patties from the mixture.

Select Air Fry mode.

Set time to 10 minutes and temperature 370 F then press START.

The air fryer display will prompt you to ADD FOOD once the temperature is reached then place patties in the air fryer basket.

Serve and enjoy.

Nutrition:

Calories 167

Fat 10.7 g

Carbohydrates 7.1 g

Sugar 1.6 g

Protein 10.6 g

71.   Summer Eggplant & Zucchini

Preparation Time: *15 minutes*

Cooking Time: *15 minutes*

Servings: 8

Ingredients:

1 eggplant

1 tomato

1 zucchini

oz chive stems

green peppers

1 teaspoon paprika

1 tablespoon olive oil

½ teaspoon ground nutmeg

½ teaspoon ground thyme

1 teaspoon salt

Directions:

1. Preheat the air fryer to 390 F.

2. Wash the eggplant, tomato, and zucchini carefully.

3. Chop all the vegetables roughly.

4. Place the chopped vegetables in the air fryer basket tray.

5. Coat the vegetables with the paprika, olive oil, ground nutmeg, ground thyme, and salt.

6. Stir the vegetables using two spatulas.

7. Cut the green peppers into squares.

8. Add the squares into the vegetable mixture. Stir gently.

9. Cook for 15 minutes, stirring after 10 minutes then serve.

Nutrition:

Calories 48

Fat 2.1

Fiber 3.3

Carbs 7.4

Protein 1.4

72.   Zucchini Hassel back

Preparation Time: *15 minutes*

Cooking Time: *12 minutes*

Servings: 2

Ingredients:

1 zucchini

oz. Cheddar, sliced

½ teaspoon salt

½ teaspoon dried oregano

½ teaspoon ground coriander

½ teaspoon paprika

tablespoons heavy cream

1 teaspoon olive oil

¼ teaspoon minced garlic

Directions:

1. Cut the zucchini into a Hassel back shape.

2. Then fill the zucchini with the sliced cheese.

3. Coat the zucchini Hassel back with salt, dried oregano, ground coriander, paprika, minced garlic, olive oil, and heavy cream.

4. Preheat the air fryer to 400 F.

5. Wrap the zucchini Hassel back in foil and place in the preheated air fryer.

6. Cook for 12 minutes

7. When the zucchini is cooked, remove it from the foil and cut into 2 pieces.

Nutrition:

Calories 215

Fat 14.9

Carbs 5.7

Protein 15.6

73.   Salty Lemon Artichokes

Preparation Time: *15 minutes*

Cooking Time: 45 minutes

Servings: 2

Ingredients:

1 lemon

2 artichokes

1 teaspoon kosher salt

1 garlic head

2 teaspoon olive oil

Directions:

Cut off the edges of the artichokes.

Cut the lemon into the halves.

Peel the garlic head and chop the garlic cloves roughly.

Then place the chopped garlic in the artichokes.

Sprinkle the artichokes with olive oil and kosher salt.

Then squeeze the lemon juice into the artichokes.

Wrap the artichokes in the foil.

Preheat the air fryer to 330 F.

Place the wrapped artichokes in the air fryer and cook for 45 minutes.

When the artichokes are cooked – discard the foil and serve.

Nutrition:

Calories 133,

Fat 5,

Fiber 9.7,

Carbs 21.7,

Protein 6

74. Asparagus & Parmesan

Preparation Time: *10 minutes*

Cooking Time: *6 minutes*

Servings: 2

Ingredients:

1 teaspoon sesame oil

11 oz. asparagus

1 teaspoon chicken stock

½ teaspoon ground white pepper

3 oz. Parmesan

Directions:

Wash the asparagus and chop it roughly.

Sprinkle the chopped asparagus with the chicken stock and ground white pepper.

Then sprinkle the vegetables with the sesame oil and shake them.

Place the asparagus in the air fryer basket.

Cook the vegetables for 4 minutes at 400 F.

Meanwhile, shred Parmesan cheese.

When the time is over – shake the asparagus gently and sprinkle with the shredded cheese.

Cook the asparagus for 2 minutes more at 400 F.

After this, transfer the cooked asparagus into the serving plates.

Nutrition:

Calories 189,

Fat 11.6,

Fiber 3.4,

Carbs 7.9

Protein 17.2

75. Onion Green Beans

Preparation Time: *10 minutes*

Cooking Time: 12 minutes

Servings: 2

Ingredients:

11 oz. green beans

1 tablespoon onion powder

1 tablespoon olive oil

½ teaspoon salt

¼ teaspoon chili flakes

Directions:

Wash the green beans carefully and place them in the bowl.

Sprinkle the green beans with onion powder, salt, chili flakes, and olive oil.

Shake the green beans carefully.

Preheat the air fryer to 400 F.

Put the green beans in the air fryer and cook for 8 minutes.

After this, shake the green beans and cook them for 4 minutes more at 400 F.

When the time is over – shake the green beans.

Serve the side dish and enjoy.

Nutrition:

Calories 1205,

Fat 7.2,

Fiber 5.5,

Carbs 13.9,

Protein 3.2

76.   Lemon Garlic Shrimp

Preparation time: *10 minutes*

Cooking time: *15 minutes*

Servings: 2

Ingredients:

1 lemon, medium-sized

1/2 lb. shrimp, medium, shelled, and deveined

1/2 tsp. Old Bay® seasoning

2 tbsp. unsalted butter, melted

1/2 tsp. minced garlic

Directions:

Grate the rind of the lemon into a bowl. Cut the lemon in half and juice it over the same bowl.

Toss in the shrimp, Old Bay®, and butter, mixing everything to make sure the shrimp is completely covered.

Transfer to a round baking dish roughly 6-inch wide, then place this dish in your fryer.

Cook at 400°F for 6 minutes. The shrimp is cooked when it turns a bright pink color.

Serve hot, drizzling any leftover sauce over the shrimp.

Nutrition:

Calories: 490

Fat: 9 g.

Protein: 12 g.

Sugar: 11 g.

77.   Garlicky Pork Belly With New Potatoes

Preparation time: *10 minutes*

Cooking time: *30 minutes*

Servings: 4

Ingredients:

1 1/2 lb. pork belly, cut into 4 pieces, rinsed, and drained

1 lb. new potatoes, peeled, scrubbed, and halved

1/2 tsp. turmeric powder

1 tsp. smoked paprika

2 tbsp. oyster sauce

2 tbsp. green onions, chopped

4 garlic cloves, sliced

Kosher salt and black pepper, to taste

Cooking spray

Directions:

Lay the pork belly on a cutting board; sprinkle with turmeric powder, smoked paprika, salt, and pepper to season. Let sit for 10 minutes.

Generously top the pork belly with oyster sauce. Arrange the belly in the air fryer basket, then spritz the belly with cooking spray on both sides.

Put the air fryer lid on and cook in the preheated instant vortex at 380°F for 20 minutes. Flip the belly when it shows "TURN FOOD" on the lid screen halfway through the cooking.

Remove the belly from the basket, and reserve. Put the new potatoes, green onions, and sliced garlic in the basket.

Put the lid on and cook at 380°F for 15 minutes or until the new potatoes are brown and crispy on the edges and cooked through in the center. Shake the basket periodically.

Remove them from the basket and serve with pork belly in a large dish.

Nutrition:

Calories: 546

Fat: 30.3 g.

Carbs: 20.7 g.

Protein: 45.2 g.

Sugar: 1.3 g.

78.   Air Fried Catfish

Preparation Time: *5 minutes*

Cooking Time: 20 minutes

Servings: 2

Ingredients:

1 whole egg

catfish fillets

¼ cup almond flour

Salt and Pepper, to taste

tbsp. olive oil

Directions:

1. Fix the temperature to 350 F and preheat the air-fryer for 5 minutes.

2. Sprinkle some salt and pepper on the catfish fillet.

3. Beat the eggs, soak the catfish in it and dip it in almond flour.

4. Remove any excess and apply a coat of olive oil on its surface.

5. Transfer the fish to the air-fryer and let it cook for 15 minutes at a temperature of 350 F.

6. *Enjoy!*

Nutrition:

Calories: 210

Carbs: 9 g

Fat: 11 g

Protein: 17 g

79.   Lemon Fish Fillet

Preparation Time: *5 minutes*

Cooking Time: 20 minutes

Servings: 2

Ingredients:

salmon fish fillets

½ cup almond flour

1 lemon

tbsp. vegetable oil

1 whole egg

Directions:

1. Fix the temperature to 400° F and preheat the air-fryer for 5 minutes.

2. Season the fish with lemon, salt, pepper and vegetable oil.

3. Beat the egg and soak the fillet in it. Cover the fillet with almond flour.

4. Transfer the fish into the cooking basket and let it cook for 15 minutes at a temperature of 400 F.

5. *Enjoy!*

Nutrition:

Calories: 230

Carbs: 10 g

Fat: 12 g

Protein: 20 g

80.   Coconut shrimp

Preparation Time: *10 minutes*

Cooking Time: 10 minutes

Servings: 2

Ingredients:

1 cup coconut, unsweetened and dried

large shrimps

1 cup white flour

1 cup egg white

1 cup panko breadcrumbs

Directions:

1. Keep the shrimp on some paper towels.

2. Combine the breadcrumbs and coconut in a pan and keep it aside.

3. In another pan, mix the cornstarch and the flour and keep it aside.

4. Keep the egg whites in a bowl

5. Put the shrimp, one at a time, first in the flour mixture. Then dip it in the egg whites and finally into the breadcrumbs mixture.

6. Transfer all the shrimp into the air-fryer basket.

7. Adjust the temperature to 400 F and time to 10 minutes.

8. Halfway through the Cooking Time, you can turn over the shrimp if needed.

9. *Enjoy!*

Nutrition:

Calories: 220

Carbs: 11 g

Fat: 10 g

Protein: 16 g

81.   Baked Mahi Mahi

Preparation Time: 10 minutes

Cooking Time: 30 minutes

Servings: 4

Ingredients:

4 Mahi Mahi fillets

1 tsp onion powder

1 tsp garlic powder

1 tsp turmeric

1 tbsp dried basil

1 tsp pepper

1 tsp salt

Directions:

In a small bowl, mix together onion powder, garlic powder, turmeric, basil, pepper, and salt.

Season fish fillets with spice mixture.

Place the cooking tray in the air fryer basket. Line air fryer basket with parchment paper.

Select Bake mode.

Set time to 30 minutes and temperature 350 F then press START.

The air fryer display will prompt you to ADD FOOD once the temperature is reached then place the fish fillet in the air fryer basket.

Serve and enjoy.

Nutrition:

Calories 108

Fat 1.1 g

Carbohydrates 2.7 g

Sugar 0.4 g

Protein 21.3 g

82.   Baked Basa

Preparation Time: 10 minutes

Cooking Time: 30 minutes

Servings: 2

Ingredients:

2 basa fish fillets

4 lemon slices

1/8 tsp lemon juice

1/2 tbsp dried basil

1/2 tsp paprika

4 tsp butter, melted

1/8 tsp salt

Directions:

In a small bowl, mix together butter, paprika, basil, lemon juice, and salt.

Brush fish fillets with melted butter mixture.

Place the cooking tray in the air fryer basket. Line air fryer basket with parchment paper.

Select Air Fry mode.

Set time to 30 minutes and temperature 350 F then press START.

The air fryer display will prompt you to ADD FOOD once the temperature is reached then place fish fillets in the air fryer basket and place lemon slices on fish fillets.

Turn fish fillets halfway through.

Serve and enjoy.

Nutrition:

Calories 293

Fat 19.6 g

Carbohydrates 5.8 g

Sugar 3.2 g

Protein 24 g

83.   Buffalo wings

Preparation Time: *5 minutes*

Cooking Time: 30 minutes

Servings: 2

Ingredients:

tbsp. hot sauce

lb. chicken wings

tbsp. melted butter

Salt and pepper, to taste

Directions:

1. Cut off the ends of the chicken wings

2. Mix the hot sauce and melted butter.

3. Let the chicken marinate in the hot sauce overnight or for minutes in the fridge.

4. Set the temperature to 390 F and preheat the air-fryer

5. Transfer the wings into the cooking basket and let it cook for 14 minutes.

6. Make the extra sauce with 3 tbsp. of melted butter and ¼ cup of hot sauce.

7. Take a plastic bag or a bowl and add the chicken wings to it. Add some extra sauce if necessary.

8. Serve with blue cheese dip or ranch.

Nutrition:

Calories: 190

Carbs: 9 g

Fat: 9 g

Protein: 15 g

84.   Spanish Pork Kabobs

Preparation time: *35 minutes*

Cooking time: *2 hours*

Servings: *4*

Ingredients:

2 lb. pork loin chop, center-cut, cut into bite-sized pieces

1/4 cup dry red wine

1/2 tsp. turmeric, ground

1/2 tsp. coriander, ground

1 tsp. oregano

1 tsp. cumin, ground

2 garlic cloves, minced

2 tsp. sweet Spanish paprika

2 tbsp. extra virgin olive oil

Sea salt and freshly ground black pepper, to taste

1 lemon, 1/2 juiced 1/2 wedges

4 skewers, soak for 30 minutes

Directions:

Place the pork loin chops in a large bowl, pour the red wine on top, sprinkle with turmeric, coriander, oregano, cumin, minced garlic, Spanish paprika, salt, and pepper, toss to coat evenly, then drizzle with olive oil. Wrap the bowl with plastic and refrigerate to marinate for 2 hours.

To make the kabobs, run the skewers through each marinated loin chop lengthwise, then arrange them in the air fryer basket.

Put the air fryer lid on and cook in batches in the preheated instant vortex at 360°F for 15–17 minutes. Shake the basket at least 3 times during the cooking.

Remove the kabobs from the basket to a serving dish, top with lemon juice, and garnished with lemon wedges to serve.

Nutrition:

Calories: 433

Fat: 24 g.

Carbs: 3.5 g.

Protein: 49.5 g.

Sugar: 0.5 g.

85.   **Simple Greek Pork Sirloin With Tzatziki**

Preparation time: *5 minutes*

Cooking time: *20 minutes*

Servings: *4*

Ingredients:

Greek Pork:

2 lb. pork sirloin roast

1/2 tsp. celery seeds

1/2 tsp. mustard seeds

1/2 tsp. ginger, ground

1 tsp. fennel seeds

1 tsp. smoked paprika

1 tsp. turmeric powder

1 tsp. Chili ancho powder

2 cloves garlic, finely chopped

Salt and black pepper, to taste

2 tbsp. olive oil

Tzatziki:

1/2 cucumber, finely chopped and squeezed

1 garlic clove, minced

1 cup Greek yogurt, full-fat

1 tsp. fresh dill, minced

1 tsp. balsamic vinegar

1 tbsp. extra-virgin olive oil

Salt, to taste

Directions:

In a large bowl, mix the celery seeds, mustard seeds, ground ginger, fennel seeds, paprika, turmeric powder, chili ancho powder, chopped garlic, salt, and pepper. Toss the sirloin in the mixture to coat well, then drizzle the olive oil on both sides of the sirloin.

Arrange the sirloin in the air fryer basket. Place the air fryer lid on and cook in the preheated instant vortex at 360°F for 20 minutes. Flip the sirloin when it shows "TURN FOOD" on the lid screen during the cooking.

In the meantime, combine all the tzatziki ingredients in a separate bowl. Leave the tzatziki in the fridge to marinate until ready to serve.

Remove the sirloin from the basket to a large serving dish. Slice to serve, with tzatziki on the side.

Nutrition:

Calories: 561

Fat: 30.2 g.

Carbs: 4.6 g.

Protein: 64.5 g

Sugar: 1.8 g.

CHAPTER 4: SNACKS AND DESSERTS

86. Spicy Chickpeas

Preparation time: *5 minutes*

Cooking time: 10 minutes

Servings: 4

Ingredients:

1 (15-oz.) can chickpeas, rinsed and drained

1 tbsp. olive oil

1/2 tsp. cumin, ground

1/2 tsp. cayenne pepper

1/2 tsp. smoked paprika

Salt, as required

Directions:

In a bowl, add all the ingredients and toss to coat well.

Press "Power Button" of Air Fry Oven and turn the dial to select the "Air Fry" mode.

Press the "Time" button and again turn the dial to set the cooking time to 10 minutes.

Now push the "Temp" button and rotate the dial to set the temperature at 390°F.

Press the "Start/Pause" button to start.

When the unit beeps to show that it is preheated, open the lid.

Arrange the chickpeas in "Air Fry Basket" and insert them in the oven.

Serve warm.

Nutrition:

Calories: 146

Total fat: 4.5 g.

Total carbs: 18.8 g.

Fiber: 4.6 g.

Sugar: 0.1 g.

Protein: 6.3 g.

87.   Roasted Peanuts

Preparation time: *5 minutes*

Cooking time: 14 minutes

Servings: 6

Ingredients:

1 1/2 cups raw peanuts

Nonstick cooking spray

Directions:

Press "Power Button" of Air Fry Oven and turn the dial to select the "Air Fry" mode.

Press the "Time" button and again turn the dial to set the cooking time to 14 minutes.

Now push the "Temp" button and rotate the dial to set the temperature at 320°F.

Press the "Start/Pause" button to start.

When the unit beeps to show that it is preheated, open the lid.

Arrange the peanuts in "Air Fry Basket" and insert them in the oven.

Toss the peanuts twice.

After 9 minutes of cooking, spray the peanuts with cooking spray.

Serve warm.

Nutrition:

Calories: 207

Total fat: 18 g.

Total carbs: 5.9 g.

Fiber: 3.1 g.

Sugar: 1.5 g.

Protein: 9.4 g.

88.   Maple Carrot Fries

Preparation Time: *5 minutes*

Cooking Time: *10 minutes*

Servings: 2

Ingredients:

1 cup baby carrot

¼ cup maple syrup

1 pinch salt

½ teaspoon thyme

½ teaspoon ground black pepper

1 teaspoon dried oregano

1 tablespoon olive oil

Directions:

1. Preheat the air fryer to 410 F.

2. Place the baby carrot in the air fryer basket.

3. Sprinkle the baby carrot with the thyme, salt, ground black pepper, and dried oregano.

4. Then spray the olive oil over the baby carrot and shake it well.

5. Cook the baby carrot fries for 10 minutes

6. Shake the carrot fries after 6 minutes of cooking.

7. Chill the cooked meal for 5 minutes

8. *Enjoy!*

Nutrition:

Calories 197

Fat 7.3

Carbs 34.4

Protein 0.7

89.   Sweet Potato Fries

Preparation Time: *10 minutes*

Cooking Time: *15 minutes*

Servings: 2

Ingredients:

2 sweet potatoes

1 tablespoon coconut oil

1/3 teaspoon salt

½ teaspoon ground black pepper

½ teaspoon onion powder

Directions:

1. Preheat the air fryer to 370 F.

2. Peel the sweet potatoes and cut them into the fries.

3. Sprinkle the vegetables with the salt, ground black pepper, and onion powder.

4. Shake the sweet potatoes and sprinkle with the coconut oil.

5. Put the uncooked sweet potato fries in the air fryer basket and cook for 15 minutes

6. Shake the sweet potato fries every 5 minutes

7. When the sweet potato fries are cooked – let them chill gently

8. Serve the meal!

Nutrition:

Calories 225

Fat 6.8

Carbs 42.1

Protein 2.6

90.   Corn Okra Bites

Preparation Time: *10 minutes*

Cooking Time: *4 minutes*

Servings: 2

Ingredients:

4 tablespoon corn flakes, crushed

9 oz okra

1 egg

½ teaspoon salt

1 teaspoon olive oil

Directions:

1. Preheat the air fryer to 400 F.

2. Chop the okra roughly.

3. Combine together the corn flakes and salt.

4. Crack the egg into the bowl and whisk it.

5. Toss the chopped okra in the whisked egg.

6. Then coat the chopped okra with the corn flakes.

7. Put the chopped okra in the air fryer basket and sprinkle with the olive oil.

8. Cook the okra for 4 minutes

9. Shake the okra after 2 minutes of cooking.

10. When the okra is cooked – let it chill gently.

11. *Enjoy!*

Nutrition:

Calories 115

Fat 4.8

Carbs 12.7

Protein 5.2

91.   Salty Potato Chips

Preparation Time: *10 minutes*

Cooking Time: *19 minutes*

Servings: 2

Ingredients:

3 potatoes

1 tablespoon canola oil

½ teaspoon salt

Directions:

1. Wash the potatoes carefully and do not peel them. Slice the potatoes into the chips.

2. Sprinkle the potato chips with the olive oil and salt. Mix the potatoes carefully.

3. Preheat the air fryer to 400 F. Put the potato chips in the air fryer basket and cook for 19 minutes

4. Shake the potato chips every 3 minutes

5. When the potato chips are cooked – chill them well.

6. *Enjoy!*

Nutrition:

Calories 282

Fat 7.3

Carbs 50.2

Protein 5.4

92.　　Corn & Beans Fries

Preparation Time: *10 minutes*

Cooking Time: *10 minutes*

Servings: 2

Ingredients:

¼ cup corn flakes crumbs

1 egg

10 oz green beans

1 tablespoon canola oil

½ teaspoon salt

1 teaspoon garlic powder

Directions:

1. Preheat the air fryer to 400 F.

2. Put the green beans in the bowl.

3. Beat the egg in the green beans and stir carefully until homogenous.

4. Then sprinkle the green beans with the salt and garlic powder.

5. Shake gently.

6. Then coat the green beans in the corn flakes crumbs well.

7. Put the green beans in the air fryer basket in one layer.

8. Cook the green beans for 7 minutes

9. Shake the green beans twice during the cooking.

10. When the green beans are cooked – let them chill and serve.

11. *Enjoy!*

Nutrition:

Calories 182

Fat 9.4

Carbs 21

Protein 6.3

93. Roasted Cashews

Preparation time: *5 minutes*

Cooking time: *5 minutes*

Servings: 6

Ingredients:

1 1/2 cups raw cashew nuts

1 tsp. butter, melted

Salt and freshly ground black pepper, as needed

Directions:

In a bowl, mix all the ingredients.

Press the "Power Button" of Air Fry Oven and turn the dial to select the "Air Fry" mode.

Press the Time button and again turn the dial to set the cooking time to 5 minutes.

Now push the Temp button and rotate the dial to set the temperature at 355ºF.

Press the "Start/Pause" button to start.

When the unit beeps to show that it is preheated, open the lid.

Arrange the cashews in "Air Fry Basket" and insert them in the oven.

Shake the cashews once halfway through.

Nutrition:

Calories: 202

Total fat: 16.5 g

Total carbs: 11.2 g

Fiber: 1 g

Sugar: 1.7 g

Protein: 5.3 g

94. French Fries

Preparation time: *15 minutes*

Cooking time: 30 minutes

Servings: 4

Ingredients:

1 lb. potatoes, peeled and cut into strips

3 tbsp. olive oil

1/2 tsp. onion powder

1/2 tsp. garlic powder

1 tsp. paprika

Directions:

In a large bowl of water, soak the potato strips for about 1 hour.

Drain the potato strips well and pat them dry with paper towels.

In a large bowl, add the potato strips and the remaining ingredients and toss to coat well.

Press the "Power Button" of Air Fry Oven and turn the dial to select the "Air Fry" mode.

Press the "Time" button and again turn the dial to set the cooking time to 30 minutes.

Now push the "Temp" button and rotate the dial to set the temperature at 375ºF.

Press the "Start/Pause" button to start.

When the unit beeps to show that it is preheated, open the lid.

Arrange the potato fries in "Air Fry Basket" and insert them in the oven.

Nutrition:

Calories: 172

Total fat: 10.7 g.

Total carbs: 18.6 g.

Fiber: 3 g.

Sugar: 1.6 g.

Protein: 2.1 g.

95.   Chocolate Chip Cookies

Preparation time: *15 minutes*

Cooking time: *5 minutes*

Servings: 18

Ingredients:

2 sticks (1 cup) unsalted butter:

3/4 cup dark brown sugar

3/4 tbsp. of dark brown sugar

2 tbsp. vanilla extract

2 large eggs

1 tsp. kosher salt

1 tsp. baking soda

2 1/3 cups All-purpose flour

2 cups chocolate chips

3/4 cups chopped walnuts

Cooking spray

Flaky sea salt, for garnish (optional)

Directions:

Take a large bowl and add unsalted butter in it. Beat the butter with an electric hand mixer. Add 3/4 cup of granulated sugar with 3/4 cup of dark brown sugar and beat at normal speed for 2–3 minutes.

Add 1 spoonful of vanilla extract, 2 large eggs and 1 tbsp. of kosher salt, and beat until mixed.

Add in increments 1 tbsp. baking soda and 2 1/3 cups all-purpose flour, stirring until it is just mixed.

Add 2 cups chocolate chip chunks and 3/4 cup of chopped walnuts and stir until well combined with a rubber spatula.

Preheat the air fryer to bake at 350°F and set aside for 5 minutes. Line the air fryer racks with parchment paper, making sure to leave space for air to circulate on all sides.

Drop the dough's 2 tbsp. scoops onto the racks, spacing them 1-inch apart. Gently flatten each scoop to form a cookie. If you like, sprinkle with flaky sea salt. Bake for about 5 minutes, until golden brown. Remove the air fryer's racks and set it to cool for 3–5 minutes. Repeat with leftover dough. Serve warm.

Nutrition:

Calories: 330

Fat: 17.5 g.

Saturated: 8.5 g.

Carbs: 42.9 g.

Fiber: 1.9 g.

Sugar: 28.0 g.

Protein: 4.0 g.

96.   Ricotta Cake

Preparation Time: 10 minutes

Cooking Time: 55 minutes

Servings: 8

Ingredients:

4 eggs

1 fresh lemon zest

2 tbsp stevia

18 oz ricotta

1 fresh lemon juice

Directions:

In a large mixing bowl, whisk the ricotta with an electric mixer until smooth. Add egg one by one and whisk well.

Add lemon juice, lemon zest, and stevia and mix well.

Transfer mixture into the greased baking dish.

Select Bake mode.

Set time to 55 minutes and temperature 350 F then press START.

The air fryer display will prompt you to ADD FOOD once the temperature is reached then place the baking dish in the air fryer basket.

Place cake in the refrigerator for 1-2 hours.

Slice and serve.

Nutrition:

Calories 123

Fat 7.3 g

Carbohydrates 4.3 g

Sugar 0.7 g

Protein 10.2 g

97.   Almond Brownie Bombs

Preparation Time: 10 minutes

Cooking Time: 20 minutes

Servings: 12

Ingredients:

3 eggs

3/4 cup Erythritol

1/2 cup almond flour

2 oz unsweetened chocolate

3/4 cup butter, softened

1/2 tsp baking powder

1/4 cup unsweetened cocoa powder

Directions:

Add dark chocolate and butter in a microwave-safe bowl and microwave for 30 seconds.

In a separate bowl, mix together almond flour, baking powder, cocoa powder, and swerve.

In a large bowl, beat eggs.

Slowly add chocolate and butter mixture and mix well.

Add dry ingredients mixture and mix until well combined.

Pour batter into the greased baking dish

Select Bake mode.

Set time to 20 minutes and temperature 350 F then press START.

The air fryer display will prompt you to ADD FOOD once the temperature is reached then place the baking dish in the air fryer basket.

Slice and serve.

Nutrition:

Calories 152

Fat 15.9 g

Carbohydrates 2.8 g

Sugar 0.2 g

Protein 2.7 g

98.   Cinnamon Nut Muffins

Preparation Time: 10 minutes

Cooking Time: 15 minutes

Servings: 12

Ingredients:

4 eggs

1/4 cup walnuts, chopped

1/2 tsp ground cinnamon

2 tsp allspice

2 tbsp butter, melted

1/2 cup Swerve

1 tsp psyllium husk

1 tbsp baking powder

1 1/2 cups almond flour

1 tsp vanilla

1/4 cup unsweetened almond milk

1/4 cup pecans, chopped

Directions:

Beat eggs, almond milk, vanilla, sweetener, and butter in a mixing bowl using a hand mixer until smooth.

Add remaining ingredients and mix until well combined.

Pour batter into silicone muffin molds.

Select Bake mode.

Set time to 15 minutes and temperature 400 F then press START.

The air fryer display will prompt you to ADD FOOD once the temperature is reached then place muffin molds in the air fryer basket.

Serve and enjoy.

Nutrition:

Calories 95

Fat 8.3 g

Carbohydrates 3.4 g

Sugar 0.4 g

Protein 3.5 g

99.   Roasted Peanuts

Preparation Time: *5 minutes*

Cooking Time: *14 minutes*

Servings: 6

Ingredients:

1½ cups raw peanuts

Nonstick cooking spray

Directions:

Press the "Power Button" of the Air Fry Oven and turn the dial to select the "Air Fry" mode.

Press the Time button and again turn the dial to set the cooking time to 14 minutes.

Now push the Temp button and rotate the dial to set the temperature at 320 degrees F. Press the "Start/Pause" button to start.

When the unit beeps to show that it is preheated, open the lid.

Arrange the peanuts in "Air Fry Basket" and insert them in the oven.

Toss the peanuts twice.

After 9 minutes of cooking, spray the peanuts with cooking spray.

Serve warm.

Nutrition:

Calories 207

Fat 18 g

Carbs 5.9 g

Protein 9.4 g

100.   Roasted Cashews

Preparation Time: *5 minutes*

Cooking Time: *5 minutes*

Servings: 6

Ingredients:

1½ cups raw cashew nuts

1 teaspoon butter, melted

Salt and freshly ground black pepper, as needed

Directions:

In a bowl, mix together all the ingredients.

Press the "Power Button" of the Air Fry Oven and turn the dial to select the "Air Fry" mode.

Press the Time button and again turn the dial to set the cooking time to 5 minutes.

Now push the Temp button and rotate the dial to set the temperature at 355 degrees F.

Press the "Start/Pause" button to start.

When the unit beeps to show that it is preheated, open the lid.

Arrange the cashews in "Air Fry Basket" and insert them in the oven.

Shake the cashews once halfway through.

Nutrition:

Calories 202

Fat 16.5 g

Carbs 11.2 g

Protein 5.3 g

101.   French Fries

Preparation Time: *15 minutes*

Cooking Time: *30 minutes*

Servings: 4

Ingredients:

1 lb. potatoes, peeled and cut into strips

3 tablespoons olive oil

½ teaspoon onion powder

½ teaspoon garlic powder

1 teaspoon paprika

Directions:

In a large bowl of water, soak the potato strips for about 1 hour.

Dry out the potato strips well and pat them dry with the paper towels.

In a large bowl, add the potato strips and the remaining ingredients and toss to coat well.

Press the "Power Button" of the Air Fry Oven and turn the dial to select the "Air Fry" mode.

Press the Time button and again turn the dial to set the cooking time to 30 minutes.

Now push the Temp button and rotate the dial to set the temperature at 375 degrees F.

Press the "Start/Pause" button to start.

When the unit beeps to show that it is preheated, open the lid.

Arrange the potato fries in "Air Fry Basket" and insert them in the oven.

Serve warm.

Nutrition:

Calories 172

Fat 10.7 g

Carbs 18.6 g

Protein 2.1 g

102.   Zucchini Fries

Preparation Time: *10 minutes*

Cooking Time: *20 minutes*

Servings: 4

Ingredients:

1 lb. zucchini, sliced into 2½-inch sticks

Salt, as required

2 tablespoons olive oil

¾ cup panko breadcrumbs

Directions:

In a colander, add the zucchini and sprinkle with salt. Set aside for about 10 minutes. Gently pat dry the zucchini sticks with the paper towels and coat with oil.

In a shallow dish, add the breadcrumbs. Coat the zucchini sticks with breadcrumbs evenly.

Press the "Power Button" of the Air Fry Oven and turn the dial to select the "Air Fry" mode.

Press the Time button and again turn the dial to set the cooking time to 12 minutes.

Now push the Temp button and rotate the dial to set the temperature at 400 degrees F.

Press the "Start/Pause" button to start.

When the unit beeps to show that it is preheated, open the lid.

Arrange the zucchini fries in "Air Fry Basket" and insert them in the oven.

Serve warm.

Nutrition:

Calories 151

Fat 8.6 g

Carbs 6.9 g

Protein 1.9 g

103.   Spicy Carrot Fries

Preparation Time: *10 minutes*

Cooking Time: *12 minutes*

Servings: 2

Ingredients:

1 large carrot, peeled and cut into sticks

1 tablespoon fresh rosemary, chopped finely

1 tablespoon olive oil

¼ teaspoon cayenne pepper

Salt and ground black pepper, as required

Directions:

In a bowl, add all the ingredients and mix well. Press the "Power Button" of the Air Fry Oven and turn the dial to select the "Air Fry" mode.

Press the Time button and again turn the dial to set the cooking time to 12 minutes.

Now push the Temp button and rotate the dial to set the temperature at 390 degrees F.

Press the "Start/Pause" button to start.

When the unit beeps to show that it is preheated, open the lid.

Arrange the carrot fries in "Air Fry Basket" and insert them in the oven.

Serve warm.

Nutrition:

Calories 81

Fat 8.3 g

Carbs 4.7 g

Protein 0.4 g

104.   Air Fryer S'mores

Preparation time: *5 minutes*

Cooking time: *1 minute*

Servings: 4

Ingredients:

4 Graham® crackers, each half split to make 2 squares, for a total of 8 squares

8 Squares of Hershey's® chocolate bar, broken into squares

4 Marshmallows

Directions:

Take deliberate steps. Air-fryers use hot air for cooking food. Marshmallows are light and fluffy, and this should keep the marshmallows from flying around the basket if you follow these steps.

Put 4 squares of Graham® crackers on a basket of the air fryer.

Place 2 squares of chocolate bars on each cracker.

Place back the basket in the air fryer and fry on air at 390°F for 1 minute. It is barely long enough for the chocolate to melt. Remove basket from air fryer.

Top with a marshmallow over each cracker. Throw the marshmallow down a little bit into the melted chocolate. This will help to make the marshmallow stay over the chocolate.

Put back the basket in the air fryer and fry at 390°F for 2 minutes. (The marshmallows should be puffed up and browned at the tops.)

Using tongs to carefully remove each cracker from the basket of the air fryer and place it on a platter. Top each marshmallow with another square of Graham® crackers.

Enjoy it right away!

Nutrition:

Calories: 412

Fat: 5 g.

Protein: 18 g.

Sugar: 6 g.

105.   Double-Glazed Cinnamon Biscuit Bites

Preparation time: *25 minutes*

Cooking time: *12 minutes*

Servings: 8

Ingredients:

2/3 cup (approx. 2 7/8 oz.) all-purpose flour

1/4 tsp. cinnamon

2 tbsp. granulated sugar

4 tsp. baking powder

1/4 tsp. kosher salt

2/3 cup (approx. 2 2/3 oz.) whole-wheat flour

4 tbsp. salted butter, cold, cut into small pieces,

1/3 cup whole milk

Cooking spray

2 cups (approx. 8 oz.) powdered sugar

3 tbsp. water

Directions:

Take a medium-sized bowl, whisk the flours together, granulated sugar, baking powder, cinnamon, and salt.

Add butter; use 2 knives or a pastry cutter to cut into mixture until butter is well mixed with flour and mixture resembles coarse cornmeal. Add milk, then stir until dough forms a ball. Place the dough on a floured surface and knead for about 30 seconds until it is smooth, forming a cohesive disk. Cut the dough into 16 pieces equal to each other. Wrap each piece gently into a smooth ball.

Coat air fryer basket with spray to cook well. Place 8 balls in a basket, leave room between each; spray the donut balls with the spray for cooking. Cook for 10–12 minutes, at 350 °F until browned and puffed.

Remove the donut balls gently from the basket, and place over foil on a wire rack. Keep it cool for 5 minutes. Repeat the same process with the remaining donut balls.

Whisk the powdered sugar and water together until smooth in a medium cup. Spoon half of the glaze gently over donut sticks. Let cool for 5 minutes; glaze again, allowing excess to drip away.

Nutrition:

Calories: 325

Fat: 7 g.

Protein: 8 g.

Carbs: 60 g.

Fiber: 5 g.

106.   **Apple Cider Donuts**

Preparation time: *25 minutes*

Cooking time: *45 minutes*

Servings: *14*

Ingredients:

For the donuts:

2 cups apple cider

3 cups all-purpose flour

1/2 cup medium brown sugar

2 tsp. baking powder:

1 tsp. cinnamon, ground

1 tsp. ginger, ground

1/2 tsp. baking soda

1/2 tsp. kosher salt

8 tbsp. unsalted butter, cold (1 stick)

1/2 cup frozen milk

For finishing and shaping:

1/4 cup all-purpose flour

8 tbsp. unsalted butter

1 cup granulated sugar

1 tsp. cinnamon

Directions:

Dough preparation time:

Pour 2 cups apple cider into a small saucepan over medium-high heat and bring to a boil. Boil until half (to 1 cup) is reduced, for 10–12 minutes. Error on the over-reducing side (you can always add a bit of extra apple cider to the reduced amount). Move the cider reduction to a measuring cup that is heatproof and cool fully, about 30 minutes.

In a wide bowl, put 3 cups all-purpose flour, 1/2 cup of light brown powdered sugar, 1 tsp. of crushed cinnamon, 1 tsp. of ground ginger, 2 tsp. of baking powder, 1/2 tsp. of kosher salt, and 1/2 tsp. of baking soda to mix.

Grate 8 tbsp. of cold unsalted butter on a grater's large holes. Add the grated butter to the flour mixture and melt the butter with your fingers until it is about the size of tiny pebbles. Create a well in the center of the mixture. Add the 1 cup reduced cider and 1/2 cup cold milk to the well and mix the dough using a large spatula.

Shaping the dough:

Sprinkle a few spoonsful of flour on a work surface. Put the batter on the floor. Pat the dough with a rolling pin into an even layer about 1-inch-thick, then add more flour with it. Fold on the dough and pat it down until 1-inch thick. Again, fold and pat, repeat the process 6 times, until the dough is slightly springy. Pat the dough into a 9x13-inch rough rectangle about 1/2-inch thick.

Cut donuts with a floured donut cutter (or 3-inch and 1-inch round cutter) out of the dough. From the first round of cutting, you will be getting around 8 donuts. Place the doughnuts onto butter paper. Collect the scraps, pat the dough down again and repeat cutting until approximately 18 donuts are in place. Refrigerate the donuts for about 10 minutes, while preheating the air fryer to 375°F.

Prepare the coating:

Melt and put the remaining 8 tbsp. of butter in a medium dish. In a small bowl, place 1 cup of granulated sugar and 1 tsp. of ground cinnamon, and whisk with a fork.

Cooking:

Air fry in groups of 3–4 at a time, flipping them halfway through, 12 minutes per group, depending on the size of your air fryer; switch the donuts to a wire rack and load the next batch onto the air fryer. In the meantime, first, dip the fried doughnuts in the butter and then cinnamon sugar. Place the wire rack back in. For dipping, serve the donuts warm or at room temperature with the dipping of hot cider.

Nutrition:

Calories: 318

Fat: 12.4 g.

Carbs: 49.1 g.

Fiber: 1.1 g.

Sugar: 25.8 g.

Protein: 3.5 g.

107.　　Mini Apple Pies

Preparation time: *30 minutes*

Cooking time: *15 minutes*

Servings: 4

Ingredients:

4 tbsp. butter

6 tbsp. brown sugar

1 tsp. cinnamon, ground

2 Granny Smith® apples, medium-sized and diced

1 tsp. cornstarch

2 tsp. cold water

1/2 (14 oz.) 9-inch double-crust pastry pack

Cooking spray

1/2 tbsp. grapeseed oil

1/4 cup powdered sugar:

1 tsp. milk, or more if required

Directions:

In a nonstick skillet, combine the apples, butter, brown sugar, and cinnamon. Cook over normal heat for about 6 minutes, until apples have softened.

Take cold water and dissolves cornstarch in it. Stir in apple mixture and cook for about 1 minute, until sauce thickens. Remove from heat the apple pie filling and set aside to cool while the crust is being prepared.

Put the pie crust on a lightly floured surface and slightly roll out to smooth the dough surface. Cut the dough into small enough rectangles to allow 2 to fit in your air fryer at once. Repeat with the remainder of the crust until you have 8 equal rectangles, re-rolling some of the dough scraps if necessary.

Wet the outer corners of 4 rectangles with water, and place some apple filling around 1/2-inch from the edges in the center. Roll the remaining 4 rectangles out, so they're slightly larger than the ones filled. Place those rectangles on top of the fill; crimp the edges with a fork. Cut 4 tiny slits into the heads of the pies.

Grease an air fryer basket with cooking spray. Use a spatula to brush the tops of 2 pies with grapeseed oil and transfer pastries to the air fryer basket.

Insert a basket and set the temperature to 385°F (195°C). Bake for about 8 minutes, until golden brown. Remove the pies from the basket and repeat with the 2 pies that are remaining.

Take a small bowl and add the powdered sugar and milk to it. Brush the glaze and allow it to dry on warm pies. Serve the pies warm.

Nutrition:

Calories: 498

Fat: 28.6 g.

Carbs: 59.8 g.

Protein: 3.3 g.

108.   Zucchini Fries

Preparation time: *10 minutes*

Cooking time: 20 minutes

Servings: 4

Ingredients:

1 lb. zucchini, sliced into 2 1/2-inch sticks

Salt, as required

2 tbsp. olive oil

3/4 cup Panko breadcrumbs

Directions:

In a colander, add the zucchini and sprinkle with salt. Set aside for about 10 minutes.

Gently pat dry the zucchini sticks with the paper towels and coat with oil.

In a shallow dish, add the breadcrumbs.

Coat the zucchini sticks with breadcrumbs evenly.

Press the "Power Button" of Air Fry Oven and turn the dial to select the "Air Fry" mode.

Press the "Time" button and again turn the dial to set the cooking time to 12 minutes.

Now push the "Temp" button and rotate the dial to set the temperature at 400°F.

Press the "Start/Pause" button to start.

When the unit beeps to show that it is preheated, open the lid.

Arrange the zucchini fries in "Air Fry Basket" and insert them in the oven.

Nutrition:

Calories: 151

Total fat: 8.6 g.

Total carbs: 6.9 g.

Fiber: 1.3 g.

Sugar: 2 g.

Protein: 1.9 g.

109.   Walnut Apple Pear Mix

Preparation Time: *10 minutes*

Cooking Time: *10 minutes*

Servings: 4

Ingredients:

2 apples, cored and cut into wedges

1/2 tsp vanilla

1 cup apple juice

2 tbsp. walnuts, chopped

2 apples, cored and cut into wedges

Directions:

Put all of the ingredients in the inner pot of the air fryer and stir well.

Seal pot and cook on high for 10 minutes.

As soon as the cooking is done, let it release pressure naturally for 10 minutes, then release remaining using quick release. Remove lid.

Serve and enjoy.

Nutrition:

Calories – 132

Protein – 1.3 g.

Fat – 2.6 g.

Carbs – 28.3 g.

110.   **Warm Peach Compote**

Preparation Time: *10 minutes*

Cooking Time: *1 minute*

Servings: 4

Ingredients:

4 peaches, peeled and chopped

1 tbsp. water

1/2 tbsp. cornstarch

1 tsp vanilla

Directions:

Add water, vanilla, and peaches into the air fryer basket.

Seal pot and cook on high for 1 minute.

Once done, allow to release pressure naturally. Remove lid.

In a small bowl, whisk together 1 tablespoon of water and cornstarch and pour into the pot and stir well.

Serve and enjoy.

Nutrition:

Calories – 66

Protein – 1.4 g.

Fat – 0.4 g.

Carbs – 15 g.

111.   Crispy Zucchini Chips

Preparation Time: 10 minutes

Cooking Time: 30 minutes

Servings: 2

Ingredients:

2 medium zucchini, cut into 1/4-inch thick slices

1/2 cup parmesan cheese, grated

1/4 cup olive oil

Pepper

Salt

Directions:

In a mixing bowl, toss zucchini slices with cheese, oil, pepper, and salt.

Place the cooking tray in the air fryer basket. Line air fryer basket with parchment paper.

Select Bake mode.

Set time to 30 minutes and temperature 300 F then press START.

The air fryer display will prompt you to ADD FOOD once the temperature is reached then arrange zucchini slices onto the parchment paper in the air fryer basket. Turn halfway through. Serve and enjoy.

Nutrition:

Calories 436

Fat 38.1 g

Carbohydrates 8.7 g

Sugar 3.4 g

Protein 21.2 g

112.   Mixed Berries Cream

Preparation Time: *5 minutes*

Cooking Time: *30 minutes*

Servings: 6

Ingredients:

12 ounces blackberries

6 ounces raspberries

12 ounces blueberries

¾ cup swerve

2 ounces coconut cream

Directions:

1. In a bowl, put all the Ingredients: and mix well.

2. Divide this into 6 ramekins, put them in your air fryer and cook at 320 degrees F for 30 minutes.

3. Cool down and serve it.

Nutrition:

Calories – 100

Protein – 2 g.

Fat – 1 g.

Carbs – 2 g.

113.   Perfect Cinnamon Toast

Preparation Time: *10 minutes*

Cooking Time: *5 minutes*

Servings: 6

Ingredients:

2 tsp. pepper

1 ½ tsp. cinnamon

½ C. sweetener of choice

1 C. coconut oil

12 slices whole wheat bread

Directions:

1. Melt coconut oil and mix with sweetener until dissolved.

2. Mix in remaining ingredients minus bread till incorporated.

3. Spread mixture onto bread, covering all area.

4. Pour the coated pieces of bread into the Oven rack/basket. Place the Rack on the middle-shelf of the Air fryer oven. Set temperature to 400°F, and set time to 5 minutes.

5. Remove and cut diagonally. Enjoy!

Nutrition:

Calories – 124

Protein – 0 g.

Fat – 2 g.

Carbs – 5 g.

CONCLUSION

Thank you for taking the time to read this cookbook. After reading this cookbook and experimenting with a few recipes, you should have a better understanding of the versatility and utility of air fryers. The use of this kitchen appliance ensures that some of your favorite snacks and meals are made in a stress-free and hassle-free manner, which invariably validates its worth and gives you value for your money.

The Instant Pot Vortex Plus Air Fryer is a cutting-edge cooking appliance that uses very little or no oil to air fry your food without sacrificing taste or texture. This makes the Instant Pot Vortex Plus Air Fryer a one-of-a-kind appliance. The Instant Pot Vortex Air Fryer is a multifunctional six-in-one cooking appliance with six built-in smart programs. It functions as a multi-cooker appliance that can air fry your crispy French fries, roast your favorite chicken or meat, broil your fish or meat, bake a delicious cake and cookies, dehydrate fruit slices, and reheat your food.

The Instant Vortex Plus Air Fryer uses hot air circulation technology to cook your food. It blows extremely hot air into the vortex air fryer food chamber, allowing your food to cook quickly and evenly from all sides. It has enough space to fry 2 pounds of French fries or roast 4 pounds of chicken at a time. You can enjoy your favorite deep-fried foods at home in less time if you use an instant vortex air fryer.

There are many things to admire about the air fryer, and it becomes an even better tool to use when you have the right recipes and can use them. And there are so many great recipes that work well in the air fryer and can get dinner on the table quickly.

Best wishes.

Made in the USA
Middletown, DE
11 June 2023

32388118R00066